MABLE HOFFMAN'S ALL-NEW

CROCKERY
FAVORITES

by Mable & Gar Hoffman

Publishers: Bill Fisher
Helen Fisher
Howard Fisher

Editors: Helen Fisher
Joyce Bush

Book
Production: Paula Peterson
Nancy Taylor

Art Director: David Fischer

Published by Fisher Books
PO Box 38040
Tucson, AZ 85740-8040
(602) 292-9080

Copyright 1991 Fisher Books

Printed in U.S.A.
Printing 10 9 8 7 6 5 4

**Library of Congress
Cataloging-in-Publication Data**

Hoffman, Mable
Crockery favorites / by Mable and Gar Hoffman.
p. cm.
Includes index.
ISBN 1-55561-046-3
1. Electric cookery, Slow. I. Hoffman, Gar. II. Title.

TX827.H57 1991   91-20000
641.5'884—dc20   CIP

Notice: The information in this book is true and complete to the best of our knowledge. It is offered with no guarantees on the part of the authors or Fisher Books. Authors and publisher disclaim all liability in connection with the use of this book.

Contents

About the Authors

Mable and Gar Hoffman, Fisher Books' best-selling cookbook team, have added *Crockery Favorites* to their long list of successful cookbooks. Their other cookbooks published by Fisher Books include *Ice Cream, Frozen Yogurt* and *Carefree Entertaining*.

Fifteen years ago the Hoffmans began a collaboration with the Fishers in developing recipes for slow-cookers. This collaboration resulted in *Crockery Cookery,* a best-selling cookbook which has remained available throughout the years and still enjoys widespread appeal. *Crockery Favorites* is a companion book with new recipes, menus and ideas.

Five of Mable's cookbooks have won R.T. French Tastemaker Awards, the "Oscar" for cookbooks. Although Mable's name appears on most of their books, Gar has been an important contributor.

The Hoffmans own and manage Hoffman Food Consultants, Inc. They concentrate their efforts on food styling, recipe development and writing. They travel worldwide gathering ideas and information about foods and cuisines.

Crockery Favorites

Crockery cooking is an important part of today's busy lifestyle. It's almost like having a cook at home —fixing dinner while you're involved in other activities. Working parents like to have dinner ready when they come home to hungry children; college students can concentrate on tomorrow's exam while dinner is cooking; and retirees can enjoy a golf game, volunteer work or shopping spree. The slow-cooker is also the ideal appliance to take in your motor home or to your summer cabin. It enables you to prepare whole meals with just one appliance, freeing you of the burden of carrying numerous pots and pans.

Hearty family-style fare as well as special-occasion dishes can be cooked while you are away. Remember that there are two temperature levels on most slow-cookers—LOW or 200F (95C) and HIGH or 300F (150C). We suggest that you use LOW when you leave an unattended cooker. If you are at home and everyone is anxious for dinner, turn the control to HIGH for the last hour or two of cooking.

Resist the temptation to lift the lid from a pot while cooking. The temperature is extremely LOW and heat escapes very fast when the lid is removed, thus requiring even longer cooking time.

It isn't necessary to stir food while cooking.

Throughout this book we have offered menu suggestions, keeping in mind ease and speed of preparation. Use them as a guide to enhance your menu planning.

Always read and follow the manufacturer's "Use and Care" booklet that came with your cooker.

For easier clean up, use vegetable cooking spray or grease the interior of your slow-cooker before adding ingredients.

Crockery-Cooking Basics

High-altitude Cooking

Most foods take longer to cook at high altitudes. If you live in an area over 3500 feet, plan on longer cooking time.

Root Vegetables

Dense vegetables such as carrots, turnips, celery root, potatoes, onions and rutabagas take longer to cook than many meats. When combining ingredients in a slow-cooker, place root vegetables on the bottom of the pot; then add meats, seasonings, other vegetables and liquid. This keeps vegetables moist during cooking and cooks them more evenly.

Dried Beans

Cooking time for dried beans varies with the specific bean as well as the ingredients cooked with them. In general, small white beans, great Northern and baby limas take much less cooking time than kidney beans and garbanzos. In some cases we suggest certain beans be cooked on HIGH instead of the low setting. Presoaking before cooking in a slow-cooker is not usually necessary, but it shortens the cooking time. Check recipes for specific directions.

Amount of Liquid

If you are a novice in slow-cooking, you will notice more liquid in the pot at the end of cooking than with traditional cooking methods. With a lower cooking temperature, liquids do not boil away; vegetables and meats are not likely to dry out. As a result, most recipes call for the addition of far less liquids.

Pasta and Rice

These products are at their best when cooked according to traditional methods or microwaved, then added to slow-cooked recipes near the end of cooking time. If cooked for many hours, they become "gummy" or fall apart.

Milk, Sour Cream and Other Dairy Products

Dairy products are delicious additions to many recipes, but in most cases should be added to the slow-cooker near the end of the cooking time. Milk usually separates and looks curdled when cooked for hours. There are a few exceptions where milk products are mixed in with other ingredients and successfully slow-cooked. We have included several that we developed.

Heat Comes From Sides of Pot

Unlike pots and pans you use on your stovetop, most slow-cookers heat from the sides instead of the bottom. Heating coils are in the outside metal shell holding the liner. When you turn it on, these coils become hot and heat the crockery liner. Others use a heating base which provides heat from the bottom. For best results, the pot should be at least half full of ingredients.

Seasonings

We omitted additional salt from recipes that call for ingredients which contain salt. Please season to taste. Experiment with using larger amounts of spices because slow-cooking produces more liquid, diluting the effect of your spices.

Advantages of Slow-Cooking

Food Cooks While You Are Away

Put everything in the pot, cover and cook on LOW. You can leave for the day and when you return dinner will be ready. LOW heat does not dry out or burn the food.

Exact Timing Is Not Crucial

If you are delayed in traffic on the way home, another half hour or even an hour of extra cooking time doesn't make that much difference to most recipes that are cooking on LOW. The temperature is so low that exact timing is not critical.

Saves Energy

These pots use very little electricity because the wattage is very low. You benefit because this is a cost-efficient method of meal preparation.

Ease of Preparation

Prepare vegetables and other cut ingredients the day before; wrap and refrigerate separately until needed.

Relieves After-work Stress

After a long day at work, the hassle of deciding "what to have for dinner" is avoided when you have dinner in the slow-cooker. And it's great to come home to wonderful cooking aromas.

Does Not Heat the Kitchen

Although many people associate crockery cooking with hearty winter dishes, we've included many year-round suggestions to help you keep your kitchen cool all summer.

Foods Are Moist and Flavorful

Slow-cooking avoids the usual shrinkage of meats. Meat and vegetable juices blend together, creating more flavorful dishes. You'll find inexpensive cuts of meat benefit greatly from slow-cooking.

Handy for Buffets

Prepare appetizers or main dishes in the slow-cooker. Keep the pot plugged in on LOW, and the food will be just as warm for the last guest as it was for the first.

You Can Take It With You

When going to a potluck or picnic in the park, prepare a main dish or vegetable at home. To transport it, wrap the entire hot, filled slow-cooker with lid in place in 2 layers of foil, then at least 5 layers of newspaper. Secure wrappings with tape. Place wrapped cooker upright in a paper grocery bag or small box. *Keep in upright position at all times*.

To Thicken Sauces and Gravy

Most main-dish slow-cooker recipes result in very flavorful juices in the bottom of the pot after meats and vegetables are removed. There are several ways to thicken these juices, then use the thickened juices as sauces to enhance the food. Each recipe indicates the exact proportion for a specific sauce. Juices are usually thickened after the meat and vegetables have been removed with a slotted spoon. In some cases, the juices can be thickened while the meat and/or vegetables are in the pot. Here are some general guidelines:

Cornstarch

After food is done, turn slow-cooker on HIGH. In a cup, dissolve cornstarch in an equal amount of water. Stir into juices in the pot. Cover and cook on HIGH 20 to 30 minutes, stirring occasionally, until thickened. Use 2 tablespoons cornstarch dissolved in 2 tablespoons cold water to thicken about 2 cups liquid.

Flour

Follow the procedure above for cornstarch. But note that the amount of flour and water are different. Use 4 tablespoons flour dissolved in 4 tablespoons water to create a medium sauce with 2 cups liquid.

Quick-cooking Tapioca

This is stirred into liquid in the slow-cooker before cooking. It thickens as the meat and vegetables cook. With 2 cups liquid, add 3 or 4 tablespoons quick-cooking tapioca.

Vegetables

In certain recipes, we mashed beans to thicken mixtures. Other times, we used potato flakes or puréed potatoes with other vegetables.

To Enhance the Presentation of Slow-Cooked Foods

- ♦ At serving time, sprinkle top with chopped fresh herbs, chopped tomatoes, green onions, grated cheese, buttered crumbs or crushed corn chips.
- ♦ For a stew-type dish, drop mounds of dumpling batter on top of cooked mixture; cover and cook on HIGH 30 to 45 minutes. See page 145.
- ♦ Spoon cooked-meat mixture into scooped-out French rolls; over toasted English muffins; in puffed pastry shells; in crisp taco shells; over soft flour tortillas; in pita rounds; over corn-bread squares; over cooked fettuccine or other pasta;

over cooked regular, brown or wild rice;
over baked potatoes.

♦ Cook meat or chicken with seasonings in slow-cooker a day ahead. Refrigerate overnight. Place in casserole. Cover with your favorite pastry recipe, refrigerated biscuits or ready-to-bake pie crust; bake according to package directions.

♦ Add pea pods, mushrooms and other quick-cooking vegetables near the end of cooking time.

To Brown or Not to Brown

When food is prepared in a slow-cooker, it does not brown as it does in a skillet or oven. It is not necessary to brown food before slow-cooking, and we have not indicated this procedure in recipes in this book. However, if you prefer the color and flavor of browned meat, poultry, onions or other vegetables, heat a small amount of oil in a skillet; add meat or vegetables and brown on medium-high heat. Turn meat or vegetables over and brown other side. Or place in broiler pan and lightly brush with oil, if desired. Broil 4 to 6 inches from source of heat until brown; turn and broil other side. Add to mixture in slow-cooker and follow our directions for the recipe.

How to Reduce Fat in Slow-Cooked Meals

♦ Purchase chops and roasts with thin layers of fat.

♦ Carefully trim all excess fat from meats before cooking.

♦ Add little or no oil or fat when cooking meat or sauces.

♦ After cooking and before serving, skim off excess fat.

♦ Cool any fatty cooked meat several hours or refrigerate overnight. Lift and discard solidified fat with spoon or spatula. Then reheat mixture on stovetop, in microwave or oven.

♦ Before adding fatty meat to slow-cooker, quickly brown it in a skillet or in the oven. Discard drippings and follow the directions for the recipe.

Food Safety

Thaw meat or poultry in the refrigerator or microwave, following manufacturer's directions. Do not thaw at room temperature.

Wash hands and utensils between each step of food preparation.

When serving, do not let cooked foods stand at room temperature more than 2 hours. Remember, keep hot foods hot and cold foods cold. Refrigerate leftovers promptly.

Documentation

Nutrient analysis was calculated using The Food Processor II Nutrition & Diet Analysis System software program, version 3.0, copyright 1988, 1990 by ESHA Research. Analysis does not include optional ingredients. The higher number is used for the range of servings.

Abbreviations

Because words like *carbohydrates* are too long to fit the recipe in chart form, we abbreviated as follows:

Cal = Calories
Prot = Protein
Carb = Carbohydrates
Chol = Cholesterol

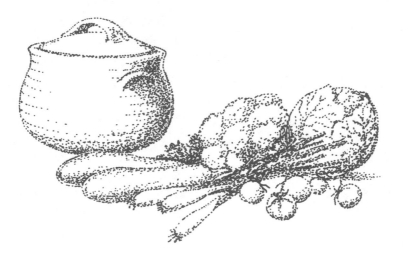

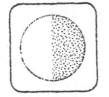

Under 6 Hours Cooking

New owners of slow-cookers find it hard to believe that there are not very many kinds of foods that can be cooked in a slow-cooker in less than 6 hours. Most of the main dishes with large pieces of meats require longer cooking time.

Ground, chopped, thinly sliced or pounded meats cook in less than 6 hours, unless they are combined with fibrous root vegetables. If you want to serve dinner within six hours, count on your slow-cooker for Apple Pork Curry, Grand-Slam Sloppy Joes or Orange-Cranberry Chicken Breasts.

Enjoy a relaxed barbecue summer or winter. Accent our tangy Smoky Barbecue Ribs by pairing them with your favorite potato salad. Add fresh herbs to your homemade biscuits or dip the tops of prepared biscuits in a butter-herb mixture before baking. Fresh fruit of your choosing is the perfect ending to this meal.

MENU

Smoky Barbeque Ribs, page 6
Potato Salad
Cole Slaw
Herb Biscuits
Angel-food Cake
Fresh Fruit

Turkey Vegetable Round

Cheesecloth holds mixture together while it's going in and out of the pot as well as during the cooking process.

1 medium potato, quartered, peeled
1 carrot, peeled
2 small zucchini, trimmed
1 leek
1-1/2 lbs. ground turkey
2 eggs, beaten slightly
1 teaspoon chopped fresh thyme
1 teaspoon chopped fresh sage
1 teaspoon Dijon-style mustard
1/2 teaspoon salt
1/8 teaspoon pepper
1 tablespoon Worcestershire sauce

In food processor, shred potato, carrot and zucchini. Slice leek in half lengthwise, thoroughly rinse and cut into thin slices. Combine shredded potato, carrot and zucchini with sliced leek, ground turkey, eggs and remaining ingredients. Shape into a 6-inch ball. Place rack in slow-cooker. Place meat on 9" x 24" double thickness of cheesecloth. Gently lift into pot on rack. Loosely fold cheesecloth over top of meat. Cover; cook on LOW 5-1/2 to 6 hours. Holding ends of cheesecloth, lift cooked meat from pot. Remove cheesecloth; cut meat into 5 or 6 wedges. Spoon drippings over wedges. Makes 5 or 6 servings.

1 serving contains:

Cal	Prot	Carb	Fat	Chol	Sodium
279	26g	9g	15g	136mg	320mg

✚ *If you don't have cheesecloth, use a piece of white cotton cloth.*

3

Apple Pork Curry

Real curry enthusiasts may want to add more curry powder just before thickening the mixture.

**2 lbs. lean pork, cut into
   1/2-inch cubes**
**1 apple, chopped, peeled,
   cored**
1 small onion, chopped
1 garlic clove, crushed
**1 teaspoon instant chicken-
   bouillon granules or
   1 bouillon cube**
1 tablespoon curry powder
**1/8 teaspoon ground
   cinnamon**
1/2 teaspoon ground ginger
1/2 teaspoon salt
1/2 cup orange juice

2 tablespoons cornstarch
2 tablespoons cold water

Cooked rice
Peanuts, chopped
Raisins
Coconut
Chutney

In slow-cooker, combine pork, apple, onion, garlic, bouillon, curry powder, cinnamon, ginger, salt and orange juice. Cover and cook on LOW 5 or 6 hours or until meat is tender. Turn pot on HIGH. In measuring cup, dissolve cornstarch in water. Stir into pork mixture. Cover and continue cooking on HIGH stirring occasionally, 30 to 40 minutes or until thickened. Serve over cooked rice; sprinkle with peanuts, raisins, coconut and chutney, if desired. Makes 5 to 6 servings.

1 serving contains:

Cal	Prot	Carb	Fat	Chol	Sodium
278	32g	8g	12g	111mg	297mg

✣ *Frozen yogurt and slices of fresh pineapple or melon make an ideal dessert after your curry dinner.*

South Seas Poultry Meatballs

A sweet-sour sauce with oriental overtones.

1/4 cup low-salt soy sauce
2/3 cup orange juice
1/2 teaspoon grated orange
  peel
2 tablespoons hoisin sauce
1/4 cup dry white wine
2 tablespoons honey
1 tablespoon sesame oil
1 garlic clove, crushed
1-1/2 lbs. chicken or turkey,
  skinned, boned, cubed
1/2 cup rolled oats
1 (8-oz.) can sliced water
  chestnuts, drained
1 egg
1/4 teaspoon salt

2 tablespoons cornstarch
2 tablespoons water

In large bowl, combine soy sauce, orange juice and peel, hoisin sauce, wine, honey, oil and garlic; set aside. In food processor fitted with metal blade, process chicken or turkey until finely chopped. Add oats, water chestnuts, egg and salt. Process until water chestnuts are chopped. Form into 1-1/4- or 1-1/2-inch balls. Place in slow cooker. Add sauce mixture. Cover and cook on LOW 5-1/2 to 6 hours. With slotted spoon, remove meat balls; cover and keep warm. Turn pot on HIGH. Dissolve cornstarch in water. Add to sauce in pot; cook on HIGH, stirring occasionally, 20 to 30 minutes or until thickened. Serve over meatballs. Makes about 30 meatballs.

1 meatball contains:

Cal	Prot	Carb	Fat	Chol	Sodium
55	5g	5g	2g	20mg	128mg

Smoky Barbecue Ribs

Use chili sauce that is similar to ketchup, not the hot spicy variety with chile peppers.

2 tablespoons balsamic vinegar

1 tablespoon Dijon-style mustard

1 tablespoon Worcestershire sauce

2 tablespoons brown sugar

1 tablespoon soy sauce

1/4 teaspoon dried red-pepper flakes, crumbled

1 teaspoon grated fresh ginger root

1/2 teaspoon liquid smoke

1 cup chili sauce

1/4 cup chopped green onions

4 lbs. spareribs, cut into individual ribs

In medium bowl, combine all ingredients except ribs. Dip each rib into sauce or brush sauce on both sides of ribs. Place coated ribs in slow-cooker. Pour remaining sauce over ribs in pot. Cover and cook on LOW 5 to 6 hours or until meat is tender. Makes 6 servings.

1 serving contains:

Cal	Prot	Carb	Fat	Chol	Sodium
542	36g	17g	36g	143mg	948mg

✤ *Balsamic vinegar has a distinctive pungent flavor; if not available use apple-cider vinegar.*

Grand-Slam Sloppy Joes

A turkey variation of the traditional Sloppy Joe; great served on warm French rolls or hamburger buns.

1 red onion, chopped

1 yellow or green bell pepper, chopped

1-1/2 lbs. boneless turkey, finely chopped

1 cup bottled chili sauce or ketchup

1 garlic clove, crushed

1 teaspoon Dijon-style mustard

1/4 teaspoon salt

1/8 teaspoon pepper

6 French rolls

Place onion, bell pepper and turkey in slow-cooker. In small bowl, combine chili sauce or ketchup, garlic, mustard, salt and pepper. Pour over turkey-vegetable mixture; stir with fork to break up clusters of turkey. Cover and cook on LOW 4-1/2 to 6 hours or until turkey is very tender. Use a fork to break up any large chunks of turkey. Cut French rolls in half and toast. For each serving, spoon turkey mixture over 2 halves of open-face, toasted rolls. Makes 6 servings.

1 serving contains:

Cal	Prot	Carb	Fa	Chol	Sodium
403	36g	48g	6g	66mg	1175mg

7

Mandarin-Style Pasta

Sauce may be cooked in slow-cooker ahead of time, then reheated and added to cooked pasta at serving time.

1/2 cup hoisin sauce

3 tablespoons low-salt soy sauce

3/4 cup ketchup

1/4 cup dry sherry

1 garlic clove, crushed

2 teaspoons sesame oil

1/3 cup sliced green onion

1/8 teaspoon pepper

1-1/2 lbs. uncooked turkey breast slices, cut into 1/4" x 1/2" x 1" strips

12 oz. angel hair (capellini) or fettuccine pasta, cooked

Toasted sesame seeds

In large bowl, combine hoisin sauce, soy sauce, ketchup, sherry, garlic, sesame oil, green onion and pepper. Stir in turkey strips. Pour into slow-cooker. Cover; cook on LOW 4-1/2 to 5 hours or until turkey is tender. Spoon over cooked pasta; toss. Sprinkle with sesame seeds. Makes 6 servings.

1 serving contains:

Cal	Prot	Carb	Fat	Chol	Sodium
464	38g	60g	6g	66mg	1061mg

✤ *Hoisin sauce is a dark, spicy, sweetened soybean, chile pepper and garlic mixture.*

Sausage-Stuffed Chicken with Pine Nuts

Flavor combinations of foods are complementary to each other.

**6 chicken breast halves,
  boned, skinned**
1/2 lb. Italian sausage
1 small onion, chopped
1/2 cup soft breadcrumbs
**1/2 teaspoon grated lemon
  peel**
1/4 cup pine nuts, chopped
**1 tablespoon minced fresh
  parsley**
1/2 teaspoon dried tarragon
1/4 teaspoon salt
1/8 teaspoon pepper
2 tablespoons dry white wine

Chopped parsley

Place one chicken breast at a time in small plastic bag or between sheets of waxed paper. Lightly pound with meat mallet; set aside. Remove casings from sausage. In medium bowl, crumble sausage; combine with onion, bread-crumbs, lemon peel, pine nuts, 1 table-spoon parsley, tarragon, salt and pepper. Divide stuffing into 6ths; form each into cylinder about 3-1/2" x 1-1/2". Place one on center of each pounded chicken breast. Fold over and secure with small skewer. Place rack in bottom of slow-cooker. Dip 24" x 14" cheesecloth into wine until moistened. Place on rack with ends extending up side of pot. Place stuffed chicken breasts on cheesecloth. Then fold ends of cheesecloth over chicken. Cover and cook on LOW 4 hours or until chicken is tender. Holding the ends of cheesecloth, remove chicken from pot. Remove cheesecloth; sprinkle chicken with chopped parsley. Makes 6 servings.

1 serving contains:

Cal	Prot	Carb	Fat	Chol	Sodium
301	34g	5g	16g	95mg	436mg

Orange-Cranberry Chicken Breasts

Popular orange-cranberry flavor combination enhances this presentation of chicken breasts.

**1 cup chopped fresh
    cranberries**
2 tablespoons brown sugar
5 slices cinnamon-raisin bread
**2 tablespoons melted
    margarine or butter**
**1/4 teaspoon grated orange
    peel**
**8 chicken breast halves,
    boned, skinned**
1/4 cup orange juice
**2 tablespoons melted
    margarine or butter**

1 orange, sliced

In medium bowl, combine cranberries and brown sugar; set aside. Toast bread; cut into 1/2-inch cubes. Combine bread cubes, 2 tablespoons melted margarine or butter, orange peel and cranberry mixture. Place one chicken breast at a time in a small plastic bag or between sheets of waxed paper. Lightly pound with meat mallet. Repeat with all chicken breasts. Spoon about 1/3 cup cranberry mixture on center of each. Roll up; skewer to close. In shallow dish, combine orange juice and 2 tablespoons melted margarine or butter. Roll filled chicken breasts in orange-juice mixture. Place in slow-cooker. Cover and cook on LOW about 5 hours. To serve, spoon drippings over chicken. Garnish with orange slices. Makes 8 servings.

1 serving contains:

Cal	Prot	Carb	Fat	Chol	Sodium
252	28g	16g	8g	73mg	194mg

✤ *When fresh cranberries are in season, buy several packages and freeze them for later use.*

Stuffed Cabbage

*Select a large head of cabbage so you'll have a number of big outside leaves.
Save smaller inside leaves for cole slaw or another cabbage dish.*

1 large head cabbage
1 egg, beaten slightly
**1 tablespoon chopped fresh
  parsley**
**2 tablespoons chopped green
  onion**
1 teaspoon chopped fresh sage
1/2 teaspoon salt
1/8 teaspoon pepper
**2 slices (about 2 oz.) boiled
  or baked ham, chopped**
**2 cups (about 1 lb.) ground
  turkey**
1 cup cooked rice

**Bottled sweet-sour sauce,
  optional**

Break off 9 or 10 large cabbage leaves.
Drop into boiling water until limp. Drain
and set aside. In medium bowl, combine
egg, parsley, green onion, sage, salt,
pepper, ham, turkey and rice. Spoon
about 1/3 cup turkey mixture on each
cabbage leaf. Fold in sides and roll ends
over filling. Place seam-side down on
rack in slow-cooker. Cover; cook on
LOW 5 to 6 hours. Serve plain or with
bottled sweet-sour sauce, if desired.
Makes 9 or 10 rolls.

1 serving contains:

Cal	Prot	Carb	Fat	Chol	Sodium
133	12g	7g	6g	50mg	229mg

✤ *For easier rolling, trim thick base of
each cabbage leaf before spooning on
turkey mixture.*

11

Fresh Artichokes

Dip tender ends of leaves and artichoke bottom into sauce or squeeze lemon juice over cooked artichoke.

2 large fresh artichokes
6 cups hot water
4 thin slices lemon

Lemon-Butter Sauce:
1/3 cup melted margarine or
  butter
3 tablespoons lemon juice
1/4 teaspoon seasoned salt

With sharp knife, slice about 1 inch off top of each artichoke; cut off stem near base. With scissors, trim about 1/2 inch off top of each leaf. With sharp knife, halve each artichoke vertically; then scoop out and discard the fuzzy center or choke. Place artichoke halves in slow-cooker; add hot water and lemon slices. Cover and cook on HIGH 4 to 5 hours or until done. Drain; serve with sauce. Makes 4 servings.

Lemon-Butter Sauce: Combine melted margarine or butter, lemon juice and seasoned salt.

1 serving with sauce contains:

Cal	Prot	Carb	Fat	Chol	Sodium
156	4g	12g	12g	0	380mg

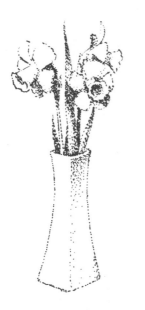

❖ *The artichoke is an edible bud of the* cynara scolymus *thistle.*

Yankee Yams

Yams are compatible with the contrast of slightly tart apples accented by maple syrup.

**2 tablespoons softened
    margarine or butter**
**5 medium yams or sweet
    potatoes**
**3 cooking apples, peeled,
    cored, cut into 8 wedges**
1/4 teaspoon ground nutmeg
1/4 cup maple-flavored syrup
**2 tablespoons melted
    margarine or butter**

**2 tablespoons chopped
    pecans, optional**

Brush 2 tablespoons softened margarine or butter on bottom and about 6 inches up sides of slow-cooker. Peel yams or sweet potatoes; cut into 1/2-inch crosswise slices. Place on bottom of slow-cooker. Top with apple wedges; then nutmeg, maple syrup and 2 tablespoons melted margarine or butter. Cover and cook on LOW 3-1/2 to 4 hours or until tender. Sprinkle with pecans, if desired. Makes about 6 servings.

1 serving contains:

Cal	Prot	Carb	Fat	Chol	Sodium
219	2g	41g	6g	0	105mg

Salsa-Topped Onions

An interesting recipe to perk up a menu of bland foods. Serve with broiled chicken or fish.

3 medium onions, peeled, halved crosswise

2 tablespoons chopped cilantro

1 jalapeño pepper, seeded, chopped

2 small tomatoes, peeled, seeded, chopped

1 garlic clove, crushed

1 tablespoon red wine vinegar

2 tablespoons vegetable oil

1/4 teaspoon salt

Place onion halves cut-side up in slow-cooker. In small bowl, combine cilantro, jalapeño, tomatoes, garlic, vinegar, oil and salt. Spoon over onions. If all onions do not fit in one layer, place 3 halves on bottom and top with 1/2 sauce. Lightly cover with heavy-duty foil. Arrange remaining halves and sauce on top. Cover and cook on LOW 5 to 6 hours or until onions are tender. Serve warm or cold. Makes 6 servings.

1 serving contains:

Cal	Prot	Carb	Fat	Chol	Sodium
58	1g	4g	5g	0	115mg

✦ *Cilantro, a member of the parsley family, is also known as* coriander *or* Chinese parsley.

Fresh Tomato Soup

Italian or plum tomatoes are ideal for this dish, but regular tomatoes may be used.

8 medium tomatoes
1 medium onion, chopped
2 carrots, peeled, thinly sliced
1 garlic clove, crushed
1 tablespoon brown sugar
1 tablespoon chopped fresh basil
1 tablespoon chopped parsley
2 teaspoons Worcestershire sauce
1/2 teaspoon salt
1/8 teaspoon pepper
3 cups chicken broth or bouillon

Drop tomatoes in a pan of boiling water for 15 to 20 seconds; immediately rinse with cold water. Remove skins. Cut in half crosswise; squeeze out and discard seeds. Combine in slow-cooker with onions, carrots, garlic, brown sugar, basil, parsley, Worcestershire sauce, salt, pepper and broth or bouillon. Cover and cook on LOW 5 to 6 hours or until vegetables are very soft. Purée in blender or food processor fitted with metal blade. Serve in individual bowls. Makes 6 servings.

1 serving contains:

Cal	Prot	Carb	Fat	Chol	Sodium
79	4g	14g	1g	1mg	279mg

Potato Leek Corn Chowder

Nonfat dry milk powder gives the appearance and taste of milk without the fat and calorie count of whole milk.

3 medium potatoes, peeled, diced
1 (11-oz.) can whole-kernel corn, not drained
1/2 cup chopped celery
1 (1.8-oz.) pkg. leek soup mix
4 cups water

1 cup nonfat dry milk powder
1/2 cup (2 oz.) shredded Jarlsberg or Swiss cheese, optional

In slow-cooker, combine potatoes, corn, celery, dry leek soup mix and water. Cover and cook on LOW 5 to 6 hours or until potatoes and celery are tender. Just before serving, gradually add dry milk powder to hot soup; gently wisk until well blended. Ladle into individual bowls; sprinkle with cheese, if desired. Makes 5 or 6 servings.

1 serving contains:

Cal	Prot	Carb	Fat	Chol	Sodium
176	8g	35g	2g	3mg	631mg

✤ *Jarlsberg is a mild-flavored Norwegian cheese.*

Caramel-Apple Euphoria

Vary this people-pleasing dessert by substituting ripe peaches for apples and 1/8 teaspoon almond extract for cardamom.

**2 medium (5 to 6 oz. each)
  cooking apples**
1/2 cup apple juice
**24 (about 7 oz.) caramel
  candy squares, unwrapped**
1 teaspoon vanilla extract
**1/8 teaspoon ground
  cardamom**
**1/2 teaspoon ground
  cinnamon**
**1/3 cup cream-style peanut
  butter**

7 slices angel-food cake
or
1 quart vanilla ice cream

Peel, core and cut each apple into 18 wedges; set aside. In 3-1/2 quart or smaller slow-cooker, combine apple juice, unwrapped caramel candies, vanilla, cardamom and cinnamon. Drop peanut butter, 1 teaspoon at a time, over ingredients in slow-cooker; stir. Add apple wedges; cover and cook on LOW 5 hours. Stir contents of slow-cooker thoroughly; cover and cook on LOW 1 additional hour. Serve approximately 1/3 cup of warm caramel-apple mixture over a slice of angel-food cake or vanilla ice cream. Makes 7 servings.

1 serving sauce contains:

Cal	Prot	Carb	Fat	Chol	Sodium
216	4g	32g	9g	1mg	67mg

1 serving with cake contains:

Cal	Prot	Carb	Fat	Chol	Sodium
341	7g	61g	9g	1mg	336mg

1 serving with ice cream contains:

Cal	Prot	Carb	Fat	Chol	Sodium
369	7g	50g	17g	35mg	133mg

Sweet Potato Pudding

Interesting dessert to serve after a dinner featuring a Hawaiian theme.

3 large sweet potatoes, cooked, peeled, cubed
1/2 cup brown sugar
3/4 cup milk
2 eggs
1/2 teaspoon ground allspice
1/2 teaspoon ground cinnamon
1/2 teaspoon grated orange peel
1 tablespoon softened margarine or butter

Whipped cream
Chopped macadamia nuts or pecans

In food processor fitted with metal blade, combine cooked sweet potatoes, brown sugar, milk, eggs, allspice, cinnamon and orange peel. Process until smooth. Grease bottom and sides of slow-cooker with margarine or butter. Spoon in potato mixture. Cover and cook on HIGH 2 to 3 hours or until mixture is puffed, firm and edges begin to brown. Serve warm or cold. Top each serving with a dab of whipped cream and chopped nuts. Makes 5 or 6 servings.

1 serving contains:

Cal	Prot	Carb	Fat	Chol	Sodium
181	4g	34g	4g	74mg	73mg

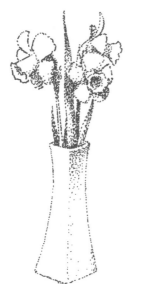

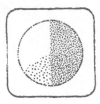

6 to 8 Hours Cooking

Within this time frame, it's possible to make our Pizza Soup with all the popular pizza flavors including sausage, tomatoes, peppers, mushrooms and topped with shredded mozzarella. Or, make a Hot 'n Sour Soup with Oriental overtones.

As far as meat dishes are concerned, Traditional Spaghetti 'n Meatballs and Beef 'n Turkey Sausage Chili will cook under 8 hours. There's time to cook Fruited Flank Steak in a spicy beer sauce.

Experience the flavors and colors of Mexico in this delightful menu. Add frozen peas to your cooked rice and cover for a minute or two to heat them. If jícama is not available, substitute fresh turnip or celery sticks. Refreshing sherbet contrasts the lively dinner.

MENU

Turkey Ranchero, page 23
Steamed Rice with Peas
Mixed Green Salad
Jícama and Bell Pepper Strips
Fresh Orange Slices
Tortillas
Pineapple Sherbet

Pork Roast with Fennel and Sage

When buying the roast, be sure that it is not longer than the inside diameter of your slow-cooker.

1 (3-lb.) pork loin roast
1/4 teaspoon salt
1/8 teaspoon pepper
4 tablespoons chopped fresh
  sage
2 fennel bulbs, sliced
  crosswise

2 tablespoons cornstarch
1/2 cup dry white wine

Have butcher cut roast through most of bone to form individual chops. Trim off most of fat. If necessary, tie roast to hold it together. Sprinkle top and sides with salt, pepper and fresh sage. Place on rack in slow-cooker; top with fennel. Cover and cook on LOW 7 to 8 hours. Remove roast and most of fennel; keep warm. Turn slow-cooker on HIGH. Dissolve cornstarch in wine. Stir into drippings. Cover and cook on HIGH 25 to 30 minutes or until thickened; stir once or twice. To serve, cut into chops. Spoon fennel over pork; then sauce over all. Makes 5 or 6 servings.

1 serving contains:

Cal	Prot	Carb	Fat	Chol	Sodium
444	50g	5g	22g	159mg	268mg

❖ *Fennel is also known as* sweet anise; *it has a very mild licorice flavor.*

Traditional Spaghetti 'n Meatballs

A good choice for an old-fashioned spaghetti dinner.

1 onion, chopped
1 carrot, peeled, chopped
1 stalk celery, chopped
1 garlic clove, crushed
1 (8-oz.) can tomato sauce
1/4 cup dry red wine
2 teaspoons chopped fresh
　basil
2 teaspoons chopped fresh
　oregano
1 teaspoon chopped fresh
　thyme
1 teaspoon Worcestershire
　sauce
1/2 teaspoon salt
1/8 teaspoon pepper
1 (28-oz.) can Italian tomatoes
　with juice

1 lb. lean ground beef
1/2 lb. mild Italian sausage
1/2 cup seasoned dry
　breadcrumbs
1 egg, beaten slightly
1/4 cup milk

1 lb. spaghetti, cooked
Grated Parmesan cheese,
　optional

In slow-cooker, combine onion, carrot, celery, garlic, tomato sauce, wine, basil, oregano, thyme, Worcestershire sauce, salt and pepper. Chop tomatoes and add to mixture in slow-cooker. In medium bowl, combine beef, sausage, bread-crumbs, egg and milk. Form into 20 to 22 (1-1/2-inch) meatballs. Carefully place in sauce in slow-cooker. Cover and cook on LOW 7 to 8 hours. Spoon hot mixture over cooked spaghetti or other pasta. Sprinkle with grated Parmesan cheese, if desired. Makes 6 to 7 servings.

1 serving contains:

Cal	Prot	Carb	Fat	Chol	Sodium
483	26g	57g	16g	85mg	847mg

Turkey Ranchero

For variety, omit corn chips and serve turkey over cooked rice or noodles. Delicious also as a filling for tacos or tostadas. Use either corn or flour tortillas.

4 turkey thighs (4-1/2 to 5 lbs.)
1 (1-5/8-oz.) pkg. enchilada
** sauce mix**
1 (6-oz.) can tomato paste
1/4 cup water

1 cup (4 oz.) grated Monterey
** Jack cheese**
1/3 cup lowfat yogurt or dairy
** sour cream**
1/4 cup sliced green onions
1/2 cup sliced ripe olives
1-1/2 cups corn chips, crushed

With sharp knife, cut each thigh in half; remove bone and skin. Place in slow-cooker. Combine dry enchilada sauce mix with tomato paste and water. Mixture will be thick. Spread over turkey thighs. Cover; cook on LOW 7 to 8 hours or until tender. Turn pot on HIGH. Add cheese; stir until cheese melts. Spoon into an au gratin dish or shallow casserole. Spoon yogurt or sour cream over turkey. Sprinkle with green onions and olives. Top with corn chips. Makes 8 servings.

1 serving contains:

Cal	Prot	Carb	Fat	Chol	Sodium
383	42g	11g	18g	121mg	346mg

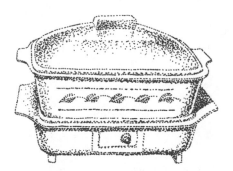

Fruited Flank Steak on Rice

Flank steak fits flat on bottom of larger slow-cooker; edges of meat will extend an inch or two up the sides of 3-1/2-quart pot.

1 (1-1/2 lbs.) flank steak
2 cups mixed dried fruits
2 tablespoons orange
marmalade
2 tablespoons brown sugar
2 tablespoons lemon juice
1/4 teaspoon ground ginger
1/4 teaspoon ground
cinnamon
1 teaspoon Worcestershire
sauce
1/4 teaspoon salt
1/8 teaspoon pepper
1 (12-oz.) can beer

2 tablespoons cornstarch
2 tablespoons cold water

Cooked rice

Place whole flank steak in slow-cooker. In medium bowl, combine dried fruits, marmalade, brown sugar, lemon juice, ginger, cinnamon, Worcestershire sauce, salt, pepper and beer. Pour over meat. Cover and cook on LOW about 7 hours. With slotted spoon, remove meat and fruit; keep warm. Turn pot on HIGH. In small bowl, dissolve cornstarch in cold water. Stir into juices in pot. Cover and cook on HIGH 15 to 20 minutes or until thickened, stirring occasionally. Spoon over warm meat and fruit. Serve on a bed of rice. Makes 6 to 7 servings.

1 serving contains:

Cal	Prot	Carb	Fat	Chol	Sodium
266	21g	27g	7g	49mg	164mg

✤ *Apple juice can be substituted for the beer.*

Meat and Potato Loaf

If Italian sausage is in a casing, remove the casing before adding to other ingredients.

1-1/2 lbs. lean ground beef
1/2 lb. Italian sausage
1 small onion, chopped
1 cup instant potato flakes,
  not reconstituted (dry)
1 egg, beaten slightly
1 cup beef broth or bouillon
1/2 cup milk
1/2 teaspoon salt
1/2 teaspoon dried Italian
  seasoning

In large bowl, combine all ingredients. Shape into a 7-inch ball. Place a trivet in slow-cooker. Place meat ball on double thickness of cheesecloth (about 24-inches square). Holding the ends of cheesecloth, gently lower meat into pot. Loosely fold cheesecloth over top of meat. Cover; cook on LOW 6 to 7 hours. Holding ends of cheesecloth, lift meat from pot. Cut into wedges. Makes 6 or 7 wedges.

1 wedge contains:

Cal	Prot	Carb	Fat	Chol	Sodium
287	22g	7g	19g	103mg	444mg

Spoon Pizza

Consider using other combinations of toppings such as fresh pork sausage, anchovies, Canadian bacon, olives, green peppers, etc.

2 (8-oz.) cans tomato sauce

2 garlic cloves

2 teaspoons dried oregano leaves

2 teaspoons dried basil leaves

1/2 teaspoon celery salt

1/4 teaspoon salt

1/8 teaspoon pepper

5 (6-inch) corn tortillas

5 teaspoons grated Parmesan cheese

1 medium onion, thinly sliced, separated into rings

2 large plum tomatoes, thinly sliced

1-1/2 oz. thinly sliced pepperoni

2 tablespoons chopped parsley

8 oz. mozzarella cheese, sliced

In blender or food processor fitted with metal blade, combine tomato sauce, garlic, oregano, basil, celery salt, salt and pepper. Process 3 minutes or until puréed; set aside. Spread each tortilla with about 2-1/2 tablespoons tomato purée; sprinkle each with 1 teaspoon grated Parmesan cheese. On each tortilla spread about 1/5 of the following: onion rings, tomato slices, pepperoni, parsley and mozzarella cheese. Place each prepared tortilla in slow-cooker, one on top of the other. Pour any remaining tomato purée over stacked tortillas in slow-cooker. Cover; cook on LOW 7 to 8 hours. Spoon pizza into a serving bowl; or with long-bladed knife, cut pizza into 6 or 8 wedges and remove wedges to a serving platter with a metal spatula. Spoon any sauce remaining in the slow-cooker over pizza in bowl or on platter. Makes 6 or 8 servings.

1 serving contains:

Cal	Prot	Carb	Fat	Chol	Sodium
181	12g	16g	8g	18mg	825mg

Smoked Sausage with Red Cabbage and Sweet Potatoes

Designed to convert the most reluctant vegetable eaters. Serve with thin slices of pumpernickel bread.

1 small head red cabbage, thinly sliced

2 medium sweet potatoes, peeled, cut into 1/2-inch slices

1 cooking apple, peeled, cored, thinly sliced

1 lb. smoked sausage ring, cut into 1-inch slices

2 tablespoons brown sugar

1/8 teaspoon ground cinnamon

1/4 cup red wine vinegar

Dijon-style or sweet-hot mustard

In slow-cooker, make alternate layers of cabbage, sweet potatoes, apple and sausage. In small bowl, combine brown sugar, cinnamon and vinegar. Pour over ingredients in pot. Cover and cook on LOW 7 to 8 hours. Serve with mustard. Makes 5 or 6 servings.

1 serving contains:

Cal	Prot	Carb	Fat	Chol	Sodium
340	12g	22g	23g	53mg	727mg

✤ *A German-inspired dish that combines wonderful flavors, both spicy and sweet.*

Lamb 'n Lentil Stew

*A stick-to-the-ribs dish for hearty appetites. Hot biscuits and a salad
complete your meal.*

**1 lb. lean lamb shoulder, cut
into 1-inch cubes**

1 garlic clove, crushed

**1 lb. zucchini, cut crosswise
into 1/2-inch slices**

**1 medium tomato, peeled,
seeded, diced**

**1 teaspoon chopped fresh
rosemary leaves**

2 teaspoons balsamic vinegar

1/2 teaspoon salt

1/8 teaspoon pepper

1 cup dried lentils

3 cups beef broth or bouillon

2 cups water

Chopped fresh cilantro

In slow-cooker, combine all ingredients
except cilantro. Cover and cook on LOW
7 to 8 hours or until lentils are tender.
Sprinkle with cilantro. Makes about
8 servings.

1 serving contains:

Cal	Prot	Carb	Fat	Chol	Sodium
203	22g	15g	7g	52mg	170mg

✜ *Make a complete one-dish meal by
adding Baked Cheddar Topping,
page 116.*

Beef 'n Turkey Sausage Chili

Sounds like an unusual combination of meats, but we hope you'll like it more than traditional chili.

1-1/2 lbs. boneless beef chuck, diced

1/2 lb. turkey sausage

1 red or yellow bell pepper, seeded, chopped

1 onion, chopped

1 garlic clove, crushed

1 (6-oz.) can tomato paste

1 (12-oz.) can beer

1 teaspoon instant beef-bouillon granules

1 jalapeño pepper, seeded, minced

2 teaspoons chili powder

1 teaspoon ground cumin

1/4 teaspoon salt

1/2 cup plain lowfat yogurt or dairy sour cream

2 tablespoons chopped fresh cilantro

1/4 cup chopped green onions

In slow-cooker, combine all ingredients except garnishes. Cover and cook on LOW 7 to 8 hours or until beef is tender. Spoon into individual bowls.

Top with yogurt or sour cream, cilantro and green onions. Makes 5 or 6 servings.

1 serving contains:

Cal	Prot	Carb	Fat	Chol	Sodium
377	35g	12g	19g	117mg	676mg

Lamb Curry

Accompany curry with chutney, chopped peanuts, raisins, shredded coconut, mandarin orange segments and chopped green onions.

1 onion, chopped

2 stalks celery, finely chopped

1 garlic clove, crushed

1-1/4 to 1-1/2 lbs. boneless lamb stew meat, cut into 1-inch cubes

1 tablespoon curry powder

1/4 teaspoon ground mace

1/2 teaspoon ground coriander

1/2 teaspoon salt

1 cup chicken broth or bouillon

1 tablespoon cornstarch

1 tablespoon cold water

Cooked rice

In slow-cooker, combine onion, celery and garlic. Add lamb, curry powder, mace, coriander, salt and broth or bouillon. Cover and cook on LOW 7 to 8 hours. Turn pot on HIGH. Dissolve cornstarch in water. Stir into cooked curry. Cover and cook on HIGH 15 or 20 minutes, stirring occasionally. Serve over cooked rice. Makes 5 to 6 servings.

1 serving contains:

Cal	Prot	Carb	Fat	Chol	Sodium
155	21g	3g	6g	64mg	239mg

Smoky Kidney Beans

Kidney beans have a very dense texture. They are at their best when cooked on HIGH.

1 lb. dried kidney beans, rinsed

6 cups water

1 medium onion, chopped

1/2 lb. smoked sausage (Keilbasa), diced

1/4 cup brown sugar, lightly packed

2 tablespoons Dijon-style mustard

1 teaspoon Worcestershire sauce

1 garlic clove, crushed

1/3 cup molasses

1/3 cup ketchup

1/8 teaspoon ground cloves

1/2 teaspoon salt

1/8 teaspoon pepper

In slow-cooker, combine dried beans and water; let stand overnight or at least 8 hours. Drain; reserve 2-1/2 cups liquid from beans. In slow-cooker, combine drained beans, remaining ingredients and reserved 2-1/2 cups of liquid. Cover and cook on HIGH about 7 hours or until beans are tender. Makes about 8 cups.

1 cup contains:

Cal	Prot	Carb	Fat	Chol	Sodium
303	14g	44g	9g	19mg	621mg

Red Cabbage and Apples

If you're using a 3-1/2-quart slow-cooker, be sure to use a small head of cabbage; a large amount of cabbage will not fit.

1 head red cabbage, thinly sliced
2 apples, seeded, chopped
1 medium onion, chopped
1 tablespoon brown sugar
1/4 teaspoon salt
1/8 teaspoon pepper
1/8 teaspoon ground mace
1/4 cup dry red wine
1/2 cup apple juice

Combine cabbage, apples, onion, brown sugar, salt, pepper and mace in slow-cooker. Pour wine and apple juice over all. Cover and cook on LOW 6-1/2 to 7 hours. Serve as an accompaniment to pork roast or chops. Makes about 6 cups.

1 cup contains:

Cal	Prot	Carb	Fat	Chol	Sodium
68	1g	15g	0	0	98mg

✤ *Our version of a classic German side-dish traditionally served with venison.*

Gingery Tomato Soup

A light soup that makes an interesting first course for dinner.

1 (14-1/2-oz.) can Italian-style
   tomatoes, coarsely
   chopped, not drained
1 (6-oz.) can tomato paste
1 garlic clove, crushed
1 red or yellow bell pepper,
   seeded, chopped
1 tablespoon chopped
   crystallized ginger
1 teaspoon grated orange peel
1/2 cup orange juice
1/8 teaspoon ground ginger
2 cups chicken broth
   or bouillon
1 tablespoon brown sugar
1/4 teaspoon salt
1/8 teaspoon pepper

1 orange, cut in thin slices

In slow-cooker, combine all ingredients except orange slices. Cover and cook on LOW 7 to 8 hours. Purée in blender or food processor fitted with metal blade. Serve in individual bowls. Garnish each with orange slice. Makes 5 servings.

1 serving contains:

Cal	Prot	Carb	Fat	Chol	Sodium
98	5g	20g	1g	0	264mg

✤ *Orange and tomato flavors enhance one another. Try this and see for yourself what a treat it is.*

Pizza Soup

Unmistakable flavors in a different form. Serve with garlic bread and a mixed green salad.

2 (14-oz.) cans Italian- style sliced tomatoes

2 cups beef broth or bouillon

1 onion, sliced

1 small red or green bell pepper, seeded, sliced

1 cup sliced mushrooms

1/2 lb. smoked sausage links, thinly sliced

1 teaspoon chopped fresh oregano

1 cup (4 oz.) shredded mozzarella or Cheddar cheese

In slow-cooker, combine tomatoes, broth or bouillon, onion, pepper, mushrooms, sausage and oregano. Cover and cook on LOW 7 to 8 hours. Spoon into individual bowls. Top with cheese. Makes 6 to 7 servings.

1 serving contains:

Cal	Prot	Carb	Fat	Chol	Sodium
188	11g	7g	13g	32mg	576mg

Hot 'n Sour Soup

A light, pleasingly spicy soup with stick-to-the-ribs ingredients.

**1/2 lb. lean pork, cut into thin
  strips**
**1/4 lb. (about 7) fresh
  mushrooms, sliced**
**1 (8-oz.) can sliced water
  chestnuts, drained**
**1/2 cup bamboo shoots, cut
  into strips**
**2 tablespoons rice wine
  vinegar**
2 tablespoons soy sauce
1 teaspoon sesame oil
**1/4 teaspoon dried red-
  pepper flakes**
**1 cup cubed firm tofu, cut into
  1/2-inch cubes**
**2 cups chicken broth
  or bouillon**
2 cups water

Green onion slices for garnish

In slow-cooker, combine all ingredients except green onions. Cover; cook on LOW 7 to 8 hours. Ladle into individual bowls. Garnish with green-onion slices. Makes 7 to 8 servings.

1 serving contains:

Cal	Prot	Carb	Fat	Chol	Sodium
108	11g	6g	5g	22mg	282mg

❖ *Bamboo shoots can be found canned in the Oriental-food section of your market.*

35

Country-Style Chicken Soup

Large proportion of chicken provides a hearty main dish.

1 (3- to 4-lb.) chicken, cut up
1 onion or leek, chopped
1 carrot, finely chopped
1/2 cup chopped celery
2 tablespoons chopped fresh
**   parsley**
1 bay leaf
1 teaspoon chopped fresh
**   thyme**
1/2 teaspoon salt
1/8 teaspoon pepper
6 cups water

4 oz. cooked fine egg noodles
**   or 3 cups cooked rice**

In 4-quart or larger slow-cooker, combine chicken, onion or leek, carrot, celery, parsley, bay leaf, thyme, salt, pepper and water. Cover and cook on LOW 7 or 8 hours or until tender. Remove chicken and bay leaf. Turn cooker on HIGH. Remove meat from chicken parts; cut into bite-size pieces. Return chicken to slow-cooker; add cooked noodles or rice. Serve when heated to desired temperature. Makes 8 or 9 servings.

1 serving contains:

Cal	Prot	Carb	Fat	Chol	Sodium
188	23g	10g	6g	74mg	183mg

Potato Leek Soup

Slow-cooker variation of a popular soup featuring potatoes and leeks.

3 medium potatoes, peeled, chopped
1 carrot, peeled, finely chopped
2 leeks, washed, sliced crosswise
1 teaspoon chopped fresh thyme
1/4 teaspoon salt
1/8 teaspoon pepper
4 cups chicken broth or bouillon

1 cup dairy sour cream
Ground nutmeg

In slow-cooker, combine potatoes, carrot, leeks, thyme, salt, pepper and broth or bouillon. Cover and cook on LOW 6 or 7 hours or until potatoes are soft. Stir in sour cream. Spoon into soup bowls; sprinkle with nutmeg. Makes about 8 servings.

1 serving contains:

Cal	Prot	Carb	Fat	Chol	Sodium
147	5g	17g	7g	13mg	93mg

✤ *Although leeks look strong, their flavor is very mild.*

Green Chile Corn Chowder

Hearty, attractive green-and-gold soup with flecks of red.

**1 (15- or 16-1/2-oz.) can
cream-style corn**

2 potatoes, peeled, diced

**2 tablespoons chopped fresh
chives**

**1 (4-oz.) can diced green
chiles, drained**

**1 (2-oz.) jar pimientos,
chopped**

1/2 cup chopped ham

**3 cups chicken broth or
bouillon**

1 cup milk or light cream

**1 cup (4 oz.) shredded
Monterey Jack cheese**

In slow-cooker, combine corn, potatoes, chives, chiles, pimientos, ham and broth or bouillon. Cover and cook on LOW 7 to 8 hours or until potatoes are tender. Stir in milk or light cream. Reheat, if desired. Serve in individual bowls; sprinkle with shredded cheese. Makes 8 servings.

1 serving contains:

Cal	Prot	Carb	Fat	Chol	Sodium
170	10g	20g	6g	20mg	507mg

Pork 'n Cellophane Noodle Soup

Good choice for an unusual soup. The noodles add extra interest.

**1/2 lb. lean pork, cut into
1/2-inch cubes**

**2 medium turnips, peeled, cut
into 1/4" x 2" strips**

**1 medium carrot, peeled,
thinly sliced crosswise**

**3 green onions, cut into
1/2-inch pieces**

2 teaspoons soy sauce

2 tablespoons sherry

1/8 teaspoon pepper

**4 cups chicken broth or
bouillon**

**2 oz. cellophane noodles,
broken into 3- or 4-inch
lengths**

In slow-cooker, combine all ingredients except noodles. Cover and cook on LOW 6 to 7 hours. About 15 minutes before serving, place noodles in a large saucepan or heat-proof bowl; cover with boiling water. Let stand 10 minutes. Drain; add to mixture in slow-cooker. Ladle into individual bowls. Makes 6 to 7 servings.

1 serving contains:

Cal	Prot	Carb	Fat	Chol	Sodium
99	10g	5g	4g	25mg	140mg

✤ *Cellophane or transparent noodles are widely used in both Chinese and Japanese cuisines. In India they are called* China Grass.

Garden Gate Soup

Apples team up with vegetables for this smooth, mouth-watering soup.

1 to 1-1/2 lbs. banana squash, peeled, seeded, cubed

1 cooking apple, peeled, cubed

1 large sweet potato, peeled, cubed

1 small onion, sliced

1 teaspoon curry powder

2 teaspoons Worcestershire sauce

3 cups apple juice

1/4 teaspoon salt

1/3 cup dairy sour cream or plain yogurt, stirred

Ground nutmeg

In slow-cooker, combine squash, apple, potato, onion, curry powder, Worcester-shire sauce, apple juice and salt. Cover and cook on LOW 6 to 7 hours or until vegetables are tender. Purée, half at a time, in blender or food processor fitted with metal blade. Stir in sour cream or yogurt. Sprinkle with nutmeg. Makes about 6 servings.

1 serving contains:

Cal	Prot	Carb	Fat	Chol	Sodium
160	3g	32g	3g	6mg	123mg

Piña Colada Bread Pudding

If you prefer to serve this dessert cold, spoon into serving dish, cover and refrigerate; then eat later.

1 (1-lb.) unsliced loaf French or sourdough bread

1 (10-oz.) can frozen Piña Colada drink mix

1 (6-oz.) can pineapple juice

1 (12-oz.) can evaporated skimmed milk

1/2 cup cream of coconut

2 (7 or 8 oz. each) ripe bananas, sliced crosswise

3 eggs

1/3 cup Irish cream or 1/4 cup light rum, optional

1 cup golden raisins

1 (8-oz.) can crushed pineapple and juice

1 teaspoon grated lemon peel

8 or 10 fresh mint sprigs

With sharp knife, peel crust from bread; discard crust or make into breadcrumbs for use in another recipe. Cut bread into 1-inch cubes; set aside. In blender or food processor fitted with metal blade, combine *half* of following ingredients: drink mix, pineapple juice, milk, cream of coconut and banana slices. Process until puréed; pour purée into 6-cup bowl. Purée remaining half of liquid ingredients and banana slices as well as eggs and liqueur, if desired. Combine both purées. Combine raisins and crushed pineapple with juice; set aside. Place about 2/3 of bread cubes in slow-cooker; sprinkle 1/2 teaspoon grated lemon peel and spread 1 cup raisin-pineapple mixture over bread in slow-cooker. Top with remaining bread cubes; then with remaining lemon peel and raisin-pineapple mixture. Pour puréed ingredients into slow-cooker. Cover and cook on LOW 6 hours. Spoon pudding into 8 or 10 dessert dishes and serve hot. Garnish with mint. Makes 8 or 10 servings.

1 serving contains:

Cal	Prot	Carb	Fat	Chol	Sodium
362	10g	60g	8g	65mg	345mg

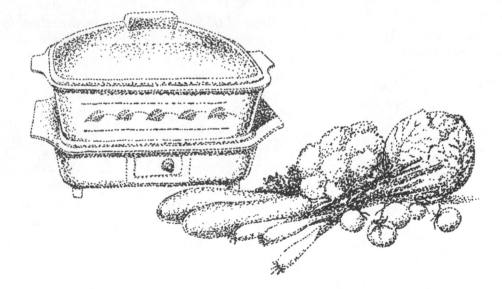

8 to 10 Hours Cooking

Tantalizing aromas will permeate your home all day if you choose a recipe in this chapter. These dishes lend themselves to long slow-cooking to bring out the maximum flavor of those tender morsels.

There's a potpourri of flavors, including several soups and stews. Also included are hearty dishes that are too thick to be called a *soup*, usually under the label of chili or stews.

A delicious wholesome stew you can serve direct from the pot. Fresh vegetables lend extra texture and color. Dip crusty French bread into the hearty sauce. For a refreshing finale serve your favorite ice cream and offer a variety of toppings.

MENU

Lamb Ragout, page 51
Sliced Tomatoes
Celery and Zucchini Sticks
French Bread
Ice Cream Sundaes
Cookies

Angel Hair Pasta Soup

For a variety in pasta, try cheese-filled ravioli or other fresh refrigerated pastas found in the deli or dairy section of your market.

1 onion, quartered

1 medium celery root, peeled, cubed

1 garlic clove

1 teaspoon chopped fresh thyme

1 carrot, peeled, quartered

1 tablespoon coarsely chopped fresh parsley

1 (28-oz.) can Italian-style tomatoes

2 oz. prosciutto ham, coarsely chopped

5 cups chicken broth or bouillon

4 oz. angel hair (capellini) pasta, broken into 3- or 4-inch lengths

Grated Parmesan cheese

In food processor fitted with metal blade, combine onion, celery root, garlic, thyme, carrot and parsley. Process until finely chopped but not puréed; remove. Repeat process with tomatoes and prosciutto. Combine chopped ingredients and broth or bouillon in slow-cooker. Cover; cook on LOW 8 to 9 hours. Turn on HIGH. Add pasta; cover and cook on HIGH 20 to 25 minutes or until pasta is tender. Ladle into individual bowls; sprinkle with Parmesan cheese. Makes 8 to 10 servings.

1 serving contains:

Cal	Prot	Carb	Fat	Chol	Sodium
98	7g	15g	2g	4mg	247mg

❖ *Capellini (capelli d'angelo), which means angel hair, is the thinnest variety of pasta.*

Lentil Chili

For an interesting change, serve over baked potatoes.

1 lb. beef or lamb stew meat, cubed

1 (14-1/2-oz.) can chopped, peeled tomatoes

1 (8-oz.) can tomato sauce

1 onion, chopped

1 garlic clove, crushed

1/2 teaspoon ground cumin

2 teaspoons chili powder

2 tablespoons chopped fresh cilantro leaves

2 tablespoons balsamic vinegar

1 cup dried lentils, rinsed

1/2 teaspoon salt

1/3 cup plain lowfat yogurt, stirred

Cilantro sprigs

In slow-cooker, combine all ingredients except yogurt and cilantro sprigs. Cover and cook on LOW 8 to 9 hours. Garnish with yogurt and cilantro sprigs. Makes 5 to 6 servings.

1 serving contains:

Cal	Prot	Carb	Fat	Chol	Sodium
274	29g	26g	6g	55mg	568mg

✤ *Lentils are available in colors varying from green to yellow, orange or brown. Presoaking is not necessary before cooking.*

Potato Shitake Soup

You may want to serve this soup without puréeing; it's equally delicious when it has lots of texture.

**1 oz. dried shitake
 mushrooms, chopped**
**4 medium potatoes, peeled
 and cubed**
1 small onion, diced
**1 cup chopped uncooked
 chicken or turkey**
**6 cups chicken broth
 or bouillon**
**2 tablespoons chopped fresh
 celery leaves**
**1 teaspoon Worcestershire
 sauce**
1/2 teaspoon salt
1/8 teaspoon pepper

Dairy sour cream
Fresh celery leaves for garnish

In slow-cooker, combine chopped mushrooms, potatoes, onions, chicken or turkey, broth or bouillon, 2 tablespoons celery leaves, Worcestershire sauce, salt and pepper. Cover and cook on LOW 8 to 9 hours or until potatoes are soft. Process, half at a time, in blender or food processor fitted with metal blade until finely chopped but not smooth. Garnish each serving with a dab of sour cream and celery leaves. Makes 9 cups.

1 cup contains:

Cal	Prot	Carb	Fat	Chol	Sodium
118	9g	16g	2g	14mg	160mg

Gingered Carrot Leek Vichyssoise

As an alternative to sour cream, add half and half or whipping cream to cooked mixture.

3 medium carrots, peeled, shredded

2 leeks, washed, sliced crosswise

3 potatoes, peeled, cubed

2 teaspoons grated fresh ginger root

1/4 teaspoon salt

1/8 teaspoon pepper

4 cups chicken broth or bouillon

1/2 cup dairy sour cream

Shredded carrot for garnish, optional

In slow-cooker, layer carrots, leeks and potatoes. Sprinkle with fresh ginger root, salt and pepper. Pour chicken broth or bouillon over all. Cover and cook on LOW 9 to 10 hours. Purée, half at a time, in blender or food processor fitted with metal blade. Gradually stir puréed mixture into sour cream. Reheat in microwave or on stovetop, if desired. Sprinkle shredded carrot on top, if desired. Makes about 6 servings.

1 serving contains:

Cal	Prot	Carb	Fat	Chol	Sodium
166	6g	25g	5g	9mg	122mg

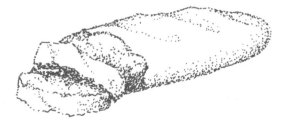

Traditional Bolognese Sauce

Spoon over any cooked pasta from spaghetti to more interesting shapes such as bow ties or spirals. Label and freeze excess sauce for another time.

1 lb. lean ground beef
1/2 lb. Italian sausage, casing removed
1 onion, chopped
1 glove garlic, crushed
1 small carrot, grated
2 stalks celery, chopped
1 small green or red bell pepper, seeded, chopped
1 (28-oz.) can diced, peeled tomatoes
2 (6-oz.) cans tomato paste
1 teaspoon sugar
1 tablespoon chopped fresh oregano
1 tablespoon chopped fresh basil
1 teaspoon salt
1/4 teaspoon pepper
1/2 cup dry red wine

Cooked pasta
Parmesan cheese, optional

Turn slow-cooker on HIGH. Add ground beef and sausage. Cook and stir until meat is broken up into small pieces. Turn pot on LOW. Add remaining ingredients, except pasta and cheese. Cover and cook on LOW 8 to 9 hours. Makes about 8 cups. Spoon over your favorite pasta. Sprinkle with grated Parmesan cheese, if desired.

1 cup contains:

Cal	Prot	Carb	Fat	Chol	Sodium
253	17g	16g	14g	52mg	746mg

✤ *Bologna, Italy is thought to be the birthplace of this versatile sauce.*

Creamy Roquefort Onion Soup

If you enjoy more texture in your soup, process cooked vegetables until they're finely chopped but not smooth.

4 large onions, cut into 8ths

2 medium potatoes, peeled, cubed

1/4 cup margarine or butter

3 cups water

2 chicken bouillon cubes or 2 teaspoons instant chicken granules

1/4 teaspoon pepper

2 cups milk or light cream

1/2 cup (2 oz.) Roquefort cheese, crumbled

In slow-cooker, combine onions, potatoes, margarine or butter, water, bouillon and pepper. Cover and cook on LOW 8 to 9 hours or until vegetables are tender. Purée, half at a time, in blender or food processor fitted with metal blade. Add milk or cream. Reheat to desired temperature in microwave or in saucepan on stove. Spoon into individual bowls. Top with Roquefort cheese. Makes about 8 cups.

1 cup contains:

Cal	Prot	Carb	Fat	Chol	Sodium
136	5g	12g	8g	12mg	510mg

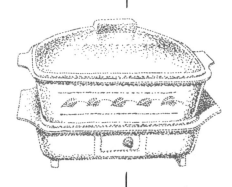

Lamb Ragout

If cooked vegetables cool while you're thickening the sauce, reheat them in the microwave before returning to the slow-cooker.

4 medium carrots, peeled, cut into crosswise slices

3 medium turnips, peeled, cut into 8ths

1-1/2 lbs. lamb stew meat in 1-inch cubes

8 small new red potatoes, halved, not peeled

1 tablespoon chopped fresh parsley

1 garlic clove, crushed

1/2 teaspoon salt

1/8 teaspoon pepper

1 teaspoon chopped fresh marjoram

1 cup beef broth or bouillon

1/2 cup dry white wine

2 tablespoons cornstarch

3 tablespoons cold water

Place carrots and turnips on bottom of slow-cooker. Top with lamb and potatoes. In small bowl, combine parsley, garlic, salt, pepper, marjoram, broth or bouillon and wine. Pour over ingredients in pot. Cover and cook on LOW 8 to 9 hours. Turn pot on HIGH. Remove vegetables and meat with slotted spoon; keep warm. In small bowl, dissolve cornstarch in water. Stir into liquid in pot. Cover and cook on HIGH 15 to 20 minutes, stirring occasionally. Return vegetables and meat to pot; serve. Makes 6 to 7 servings.

1 serving contains:

Cal	Prot	Carb	Fat	Chol	Sodium
248	23g	22g	6g	65mg	253mg

✤ Ragout *is the French term for a stew.*

Fresh Vegetable Soup with Pasta

Thanks to a variety of fresh vegetables, this is a nutritious as well as good-tasting soup.

1 medium onion, chopped

2 carrots, peeled, thinly sliced

2 zucchini, sliced

2 medium tomatoes, peeled, seeded, chopped

2 (10-1/2-oz.) cans condensed beef broth

2 cups water

2 tablespoons chopped fresh parsley

1 tablespoon chopped fresh oregano

1/2 cup small shell-shaped pasta

Grated Parmesan cheese

In slow-cooker, combine onion, carrots, zucchini, tomatoes, condensed beef broth, water, parsley and oregano. Cover and cook on LOW 8 to 9 hours or until vegetables are tender. Turn on HIGH. Add pasta; cover and cook on HIGH 20 minutes or until pasta is tender. Ladle into serving bowls; sprinkle with cheese. Makes 6 or 7 servings.

1 serving contains:

Cal	Prot	Carb	Fat	Chol	Sodium
61	3g	12g	1g	0	275mg

Southwestern Black Bean Soup

A hearty soup enhanced by the flavor of ham.

1 lb. dried black beans, rinsed
6 cups beef broth or bouillon
1 large onion, chopped
2 jalapeño peppers, seeded,
  chopped
1 garlic clove, crushed
1 teaspoon ground cumin
1 teaspoon ground oregano
1 teaspoon ground thyme
1/8 teaspoon ground cloves
2 (about 1-lb. each) ham hocks

1/3 cup dairy sour cream
  or plain yogurt
1 large tomato, chopped

In slow-cooker, combine dried beans, broth or bouillon, onions, jalapeño peppers, garlic, cumin, oregano, thyme, cloves and ham hocks. Cover and cook on LOW 9 to 10 hours or until beans are tender. Remove ham hocks; cool. Shred lean meat; discard skin, bones and fat. Return shredded lean ham to pot and reheat on HIGH, if necessary. Spoon mixture into individual soup bowls.

Top each with sour cream and chopped tomato. Makes 6 to 8 servings.

1 serving contains:

Cal	Prot	Carb	Fat	Chol	Sodium
233	17g	29g	6g	15mg	247mg

✚ *In Puerto Rico, black bean soup is traditionally served with a dash of vinegar and a garnish of white rice and chopped egg.*

Adriatic Cabbage Soup

A sprinkle of grated Romano cheese gives a classy finishing touch.

1/4 lb. salami, diced

1 carrot, peeled, finely chopped

1 garlic clove, crushed

3/4 cup diced ham

1 tablespoon white wine vinegar

1 cup thinly sliced fennel with some tops

4 cups water

1 small head (about 6 cups) savoy cabbage, thinly sliced

In slow-cooker, combine salami, carrot, garlic, ham, vinegar, fennel and water. Cover and cook on LOW 8 to 10 hours. Turn pot on HIGH; add cabbage. Cover and cook on HIGH 30 minutes or until cabbage is tender. Makes about 6 servings.

1 serving contains:

Cal	Prot	Carb	Fat	Chol	Sodium
104	9g	7g	5g	21mg	492mg

Today's Beef Stew

Take advantage of the opportunity to use tender baby carrots, tiny white onions and unpeeled new potatoes.

10 (about 1/2 lb.) small new potatoes, halved but not peeled

12 small white onions, peeled

30 (about 1/2 lb.) baby carrots

1 red or green bell pepper, cut into 1-inch pieces

1-1/2 lbs. beef stew meat, cut into 1- to 1-1/2-inch cubes

2 cups beef broth or bouillon

2 teaspoons chopped fresh oregano leaves

1/4 teaspoon paprika

1 tablespoon chopped fresh parsley

1 tablespoon Worcestershire sauce

1/2 teaspoon salt

1/8 teaspoon pepper

3 tablespoons cornstarch

3 tablespoons cold water

Place potatoes, onions and baby carrots in slow-cooker. Add bell pepper and beef. In small bowl, combine broth or bouillon, oregano, paprika, parsley, Worcestershire sauce, salt and pepper. Pour over meat and vegetables. Cover and cook on LOW 9 to 10 hours. Turn pot on HIGH. In small bowl, dissolve cornstarch in water; stir into cooked stew mixture. Cover and cook on HIGH 15 to 20 minutes or until thickened, stirring occasionally. Makes 6 or 7 servings.

1 serving contains:

Cal	Prot	Carb	Fat	Chol	Sodium
229	25g	15g	7g	70mg	303mg

Lentil 'n Ham Pot

A wholesome main dish that's ideal for a cold day.

2 (about 8 to 10 oz. each) ham hocks

3 cups chicken broth or bouillon

2 cups water

1 small celery root, cut into 2" x 1/2" x 1/4" slices

2 medium carrots, peeled, thinly sliced

1 leek, washed, sliced crosswise

1/2 small head cabbage, sliced

1 (8-oz.) can tomato sauce

1 garlic clove, crushed

1 teaspoon paprika

1 teaspoon chopped fresh marjoram

1/8 teaspoon pepper

1 cup dried lentils, rinsed

1/2 cup plain yogurt

In slow-cooker, combine all ingredients except yogurt. Cover and cook on LOW 9 to 10 hours or until vegetables and lentils are tender. Remove ham hocks; cool. Discard skin, bones and fat; cut lean meat into small pieces. Return lean meat to pot and reheat on HIGH, if necessary. Spoon into individual bowls; top with yogurt. Makes about 8 servings.

1 serving contains:

Cal	Prot	Carb	Fat	Chol	Sodium
186	15g	24g	4g	12mg	444mg

Spicy Kumquat Relish

A special recipe designed for a 1-quart Crock-Ette®, If you double or triple the recipe and cook in larger cooker, make sure the pot is half full.

**2 cups (about 10 oz.)
  kumquats, sliced crosswise**

1/2 cup dried apple chips

**2 tablespoons thinly sliced
  crystallized ginger**

3/4 cup brown sugar

2 tablespoons honey

1/4 teaspoon ground allspice

2 tablespoons cider vinegar

1/4 cup golden raisins

**1/4 teaspoon dried
  red-pepper flakes**

**1/2 cup coarsely chopped
  dried apricots**

In 1-quart slow-cooker, combine all ingredients. Cover and cook on LOW 8 to 9 hours. Cool; serve as an accompaniment to pork or chicken. Makes about 2 cups.

1 tablespoon contains:

Cal	Prot	Carb	Fat	Chol	Sodium
44	0	12g	0	0	5mg

✤ *Wrap fresh kumquats in plastic and store in your refrigerator for weeks.*

Over 10 Hours Cooking

Dried beans are associated with long cooking, and some varieties take longer than others. Larger and/or more dense shapes take the maximum time to become tender. We've made preparation easier by omitting the conventional overnight soaking. This worked well, with the exception of recipes having a high sugar content. Note that Sweet-Hot Bean Casserole, one of our favorites, requires overnight soaking *before* slow cooking. For higher altitudes, you may find presoaking reduces cooking time.

Slow-cookers are ideal for making stock, so we included the basic three.

There are times when you want to savor the taste of plain foods at their best. Here is our version of the classic New England boiled dinner. The crunchy salad contrasts the tender vegetables. Old-fashioned blueberry cobbler adds the final touch.

MENU

Tomato-juice Cocktail
New England "Boiled" Dinner,
page 65
Mustard and Horseradish
Waldorf Salad
Hot Rolls
Blueberry Cobbler

Traditional Baked Beans

Good old-fashioned baked beans without soaking ahead of time.

1 lb. dried small white beans, rinsed

4-1/2 cups water

1/3 cup molasses

1/4 cup brown sugar

1 onion, chopped

1/4 lb. salt pork, cut into 1-inch cubes

1 tablespoon Dijon-style mustard

1/2 teaspoon salt

In slow-cooker, combine all ingredients. Cover and cook on LOW 13 to 14 hours, stirring occasionally, if possible. Makes 6 to 8 servings.

1 serving contains:

Cal	Prot	Carb	Fat	Chol	Sodium
299	15g	44g	8g	12mg	391mg

✛ *For added nutrition serve protein-rich beans with a grain such as rice or a multigrain or corn bread.*

Amalfi Garbanzo Stew

If possible, use fresh basil and thyme for flavor dividends.

**1 lb. dried garbanzo beans,
   rinsed**

5 cups water

1 (6-oz.) can tomato paste

1/2 cup dry white wine

**1 tablespoon chopped fresh
   basil or 1 teaspoon dried**

1 garlic clove, crushed

**2 carrots, peeled, sliced
   crosswise**

**1 teaspoon fresh thyme
   or 1/4 teaspoon dried**

**1 green or yellow bell pepper,
   seeded, sliced**

1/2 teaspoon salt

1/8 teaspoon pepper

**4 thin slices pepperoni,
   chopped**

**3 chicken breast halves,
   boned, skinned, cut into
   1/2" x 1" pieces**

**1 cup (4 oz.) shredded
   mozzarella cheese**

In slow-cooker, combine dried beans, water, tomato paste, wine, basil, garlic, carrots, thyme, bell peppers, salt, pepper, pepperoni and chicken. Cover and cook on LOW 10 to 12 hours or until beans are tender. Spoon into individual bowls. Sprinkle with cheese. Makes 6 to 8 servings.

1 serving contains:

Cal	Prot	Carb	Fat	Chol	Sodium
301	20g	38g	7g	23mg	296mg

✤ *Serve a crusty bread with this
delicious Italian stew.*

Country Lima Bean & Cabbage Soup

High in fiber and low in fat, a robust dish.

**1 lb. dried baby lima beans,
   rinsed**
**8 cups chicken broth
   or bouillon**
1 onion, chopped
**1 teaspoon chopped fresh
   marjoram**
1 garlic clove, crushed
**1/2 teaspoon dried
   red-pepper flakes, crushed**
1/2 teaspoon salt
1/8 teaspoon pepper
3 cups shredded cabbage

In slow-cooker, combine all ingredients. Cover and cook on LOW 10 to 11 hours or until beans are tender. Ladle into individual bowls. Makes 8 to 9 servings.

1 serving contains:

Cal	Prot	Carb	Fat	Chol	Sodium
144	12g	21g	2g	1mg	125mg

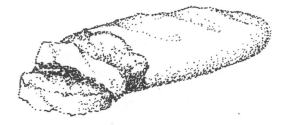

Sweet-Hot Bean Casserole

If possible, stir the beans once while they are cooking.

1 lb. dried great Northern
  beans, rinsed

6 cups water

1 cup crushed gingersnaps
  (about 16)

2 tablespoons sweet-hot
  mustard

1 tablespoon Worcestershire
  sauce

1/2 cup molasses

3 green onions, chopped

1/2 teaspoon salt

1/8 teaspoon pepper

In slow-cooker, combine dried beans and water; let stand overnight or at least 8 hours. Drain; reserve 2-1/2 cups liquid from beans. In slow-cooker, combine drained beans, reserved liquid, crushed gingersnaps, mustard, Worcestershire sauce, molasses, green onions, salt and pepper. Cover and cook on LOW about 10 hours. Makes 6 to 7 servings.

1 serving contains:

Cal	Prot	Carb	Fat	Chol	Sodium
339	12g	58g	7g	8mg	345mg

✤ *Crushed gingersnaps help create a marvelous sauce.*

New England "Boiled" Dinner

Serve this traditional corned-beef dinner in the pot along with your favorite horseradish and mustard. You'll need a 4-quart or larger pot for this recipe or use less vegetables in a smaller pot.

6 medium carrots, peeled, cut into 1-inch lengths

6 medium potatoes, peeled, quartered

2 turnips or parsnips, peeled, cut into 8ths

2 large onions, peeled, quartered

1 (2- to 3-lbs.) corned-beef brisket

5 cups water

1 small head cabbage, cut into 6 wedges

In slow-cooker, combine carrots, potatoes, turnips or parsnips and onions. Top with corned beef, fat-side up. Pour water over all. Cover and cook on LOW 10 to 11 hours or until meat is tender. Remove cooked meat and vegetables; keep warm. Turn pot on HIGH; add cabbage. Cover and cook on HIGH 20 to 30 minutes or until cabbage is done. Lift cabbage with slotted spoon. Arrange on large platter with corned beef and other vegetables. Makes 6 servings.

1 serving contains:

Cal	Prot	Carb	Fat	Chol	Sodium
406	43g	39g	9g	92mg	140mg

Pork Garbanzo Meal-in-a-Pot

Just toss everything in the pot and forget about it until dinner time.
These ingredients almost reach the top of a 3-1/2-quart slow-cooker but
will cook perfectly.

1 lb. dried garbanzo beans,
   rinsed

3 cups chicken broth
   or bouillon

3 cups water

4 large tomatoes, peeled,
   seeded, chopped

3/4 lb. lean pork, cut into
   1/2-inch cubes

3 oz. prosciutto, chopped

1 onion, chopped

1 garlic clove, crushed

1 yellow or green bell pepper,
   seeded, chopped

2 teaspoons chopped fresh
   basil

1/2 teaspoon salt

1/8 teaspoon pepper

1 cup torn fresh spinach

In slow-cooker, combine all ingredients. Cover and cook on LOW 10 to 11 hours or until beans are tender. Makes about 8 servings.

1 serving contains:

Cal	Prot	Carb	Fat	Chol	Sodium
307	25g	36g	8g	38mg	322mg

✤ *Garbanzo beans are also known as* chick peas, cei *or* chana dol. *They're a staple in Middle Eastern, European and Oriental diets.*

Basic Chicken Stock

You can freeze this flavorful stock in 1- or 2-cup containers for later use in casseroles or soup.

3 lbs. chicken necks, backs or wings

2 carrots, peeled, finely chopped

2 leeks, finely chopped

2 stalks celery with leaves, finely chopped

5 or 6 whole black peppercorns

1/4 cup loosely packed watercress

1 teaspoon fresh tarragon leaves

1 teaspoon salt

2 quarts water

Arrange chicken in single layer in shallow roasting pan. Bake in 325F (165C) oven about 1 hour or until brown, turning pieces as they brown. Transfer browned chicken to slow-cooker. Add remaining ingredients. Cover and cook on LOW 10 to 12 hours or until vegetables are very tender. Strain broth through fine sieve; discard vegetables and chicken. Refrigerate stock until cold; remove fat, if desired. Makes about 7 cups.

1 cup contains:

Cal	Prot	Carb	Fat	Chol	Sodium
39	5g	1g	1g	1mg	305mg

✚ *If watercress is not available use fresh parsley.*

67

Beef Stock

Use bones with a small amount of meat on them to ensure a better beef flavor.

3 lbs. beef bones

**2 carrots, peeled, finely
chopped**

1 medium onion, chopped

**2 stalks celery with leaves,
finely chopped**

2 bay leaves

1 teaspoon fresh thyme leaves

5 or 6 black peppercorns

1/2 teaspoon salt

2 quarts water

Arrange single layer of bones in shallow roasting pan. Bake in 325F (165C) oven about 1 hour or until brown, turning bones as they brown. Transfer browned bones to slow-cooker. Add remaining ingredients. Cover and cook on LOW 10 to 12 hours or until vegetables are very tender. Strain broth through fine strainer; discard herbs, vegetables, bones and meat. Refrigerate stock until cold; remove fat, if desired. Makes about 7 cups.

1 cup contains:

Cal	Prot	Carb	Fat	Chol	Sodium
16	3g	0	1g	1mg	152mg

❖ *Roasting the bones beforehand gives
the stock a rich deep color and better
flavor.*

Vegetarian Stock

Add a cup or two of this basic stock to intensify flavors of a vegetable sauce.

3 carrots, peeled, finely chopped

1 large leek, finely chopped

2 stalks celery with leaves, finely chopped

2 parsnips, peeled, finely chopped

1/2 cup loosely packed parsley leaves

1/4 cup loosely packed watercress leaves

6 mushrooms, chopped

2 quarts water

1/2 teaspoon salt

1/2 teaspoon black peppercorns

In slow-cooker, combine all ingredients. Cover and cook on LOW 10 to 12 hours or until vegetables are very tender. Strain broth through a fine strainer; discard vegetables. Makes about 7 cups.

1 cup contains:

Cal	Prot	Carb	Fat	Chol	Sodium
34	1g	7g	0	0	72mg

❖ *To prevent bubbling over, do not fill slow-cooker to the brim.*

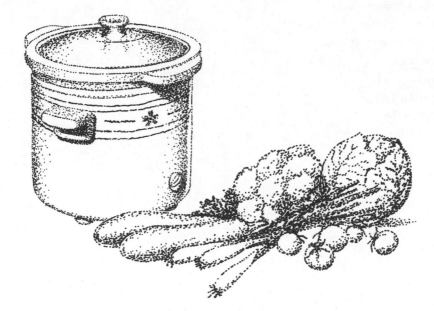

Slow-Cooker Entertaining

While you're busy with last-minute chores before entertaining, your slow-cooker continues cooking unattended. It could be cooking a new hot appetizer or an exciting main dish. Or it will keep foods warm that you've cooked in the microwave or on the stovetop. You can rest assured that the food will be just as warm for the last guest as it was for the first.

The crockery-cooker makes an excellent serving container for hot punch or cider during a holiday open house or for Halloween revelers.

It's possible to prepare festive, long-cooking fare the day before a party. Refrigerate the food overnight; then reheat it and keep it in a warm (on LOW) slow-cooker throughout a buffet or cocktail party.

Entertaining is a pleasure when your slow-cooker is working for you. Enjoy a delicious Italian dinner with a minimum of effort. Prepare the salad the day before and serve it well chilled. The Sicilian Hens on Fettuccine are sure to please family and guests alike.

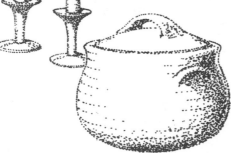

MENU

Antipasto Bean Salad, page 126
Sicilian Hens on Fettuccine,
page 76
Steamed Broccoli
Garlic Bread
Strawberries and Cantaloupe

Turkey Marsala with Vegetables

If your slow-cooker is large enough to accommodate a whole turkey breast, consider it for a larger get-together.

3 large carrots, peeled, julienned

2 leeks, washed, julienned

1/2 (about 3 lbs.) turkey breast, skinned

2 tablespoons melted margarine or butter

12 mushrooms, sliced

1/2 teaspoon salt

1/8 teaspoon pepper

2 tablespoons chopped fresh parsley

3/4 cup chicken broth or bouillon

1/2 cup Marsala or dry sherry

2 tablespoons cornstarch

2 tablespoons cold water

Place carrots and leeks in slow-cooker. Brush turkey breast with melted margarine or butter. Arrange turkey, then mushrooms over vegetables. Sprinkle with salt, pepper and parsley. Pour broth or bouillon and wine over all. Cover and cook on LOW 6 to 7 hours. Remove turkey and vegetables with slotted spoon; cover and keep warm. Turn pot on HIGH. Dissolve cornstarch in water. Stir into juices in pot. Cover and cook on HIGH 15 to 20 minutes or until thickened, stirring occasionally. Slice turkey; arrange on center of platter with vegetables around edges. Serve with Marsala sauce. Makes 5 or 6 servings.

1 serving contains:

Cal	Prot	Carb	Fat	Chol	Sodium
287	36g	13g	7g	79mg	321mg

Peppercorn Pork

When you purchase the pork roast, consider the size of your slow-cooker.
Some large roasts do not fit into a 3-1/2 quart pot.

2 tablespoons drained green
   peppercorns
3 tablespoons sweet-hot
   mustard
1 teaspoon horseradish
1/2 teaspoon grated lemon
   peel
1/4 teaspoon salt
3-1/2 to 4 lbs. lean pork roast
1 cup apple cider

1/4 cup cold water
3 tablespoons cornstarch
1 apple, cored, cut into thin
   wedges

In small bowl, combine peppercorns, mustard, horseradish, lemon peel and salt. Spread on top and sides of pork roast. Place metal rack in bottom of slow-cooker; pour in cider. Place coated pork roast on rack in slow-cooker. Cover and cook on LOW 9 to 10 hours. Then turn slow-cooker on HIGH. Remove pork and rack; cover and keep warm. In small bowl, combine water and cornstarch; stir until smooth. Add to drippings in pot. Cook on HIGH 20 to 30 minutes or until thickened, stirring occasionally. Slice roast; garnish with apple wedges. Serve pork with sauce. Makes 6 to 8 servings.

1 serving contains:

Cal	Prot	Carb	Fat	Chol	Sodium
396	44g	8g	20g	139mg	240mg

Flank Steak Pinwheels

Smaller slow-cookers (3-1/2- or 4-quart) are the ideal size for this recipe.

1 (about 1-1/2-lbs.) beef flank
    steak
2 tablespoons chutney
1 tablespoon soy sauce
1 tablespoon white wine
    vinegar
1 tablespoon vegetable oil
1 garlic clove, crushed
1/4 teaspoon salt
1/8 teaspoon pepper

Cooked rice or noodles

Trim all fat off flank steak; cut into 8 crosswise strips. Roll up; secure with small wooden pick. Place in bottom of slow-cooker. In small bowl, combine chutney, soy sauce, vinegar, oil, garlic, salt and pepper. Spoon over steak pinwheels. Cover and cook on LOW about 6 hours or until tender. Remove wooden picks. Serve pinwheels and the meat juices over cooked rice or noodles. Makes 8 steak pinwheels.

1 pinwheel contains:

Cal	Prot	Carb	Fat	Chol	Sodium
150	17g	1g	8g	43mg	281mg

Sicilian Hens on Fettuccine

*For a change of pace, impress your guests with this dish with an
Italian accent.*

1/4 cup toasted sliced almonds
3 tablespoons drained capers
3 tablespoons chopped fresh
  parsley
1 garlic clove, chopped
1/2 teaspoon paprika
2 teaspoons olive or vegetable
  oil
1/2 teaspoon salt
1/8 teaspoon pepper
2 Cornish hens, thawed,
  halved

Cooked fettuccine
Chopped ripe olives

In food processor fitted with metal blade,
combine almonds, capers, parsley, garlic,
paprika, oil, salt and pepper. Process
until finely chopped but not puréed.
Pat mixture on all sides of Cornish hens.
Place on rack in slow-cooker. If all hens
do not fit on rack, place 2 halves on rack;
lightly cover with heavy-duty foil.
Arrange remaining halves on top of foil.
Cover and cook on LOW 7 to 8 hours.
Serve on fettuccine; sprinkle with
chopped ripe olives. Makes 4 servings.

1 serving contains:

Cal	Prot	Carb	Fat	Chol	Sodium
234	32g	1g	11g	94mg	484mg

❖ *Capers are the pickled flower buds of
Mediterranean shrubs; they vary in
size and color.*

Herb-Stuffed Turkey Breast

Extra sprigs of fresh thyme and parsley make attractive garnishes for cooked turkey slices.

1 (2-1/4- to 2-1/2-lbs.) half
   turkey breast, boned, with
   skin
1 tablespoon Dijon-style
   mustard
6 thin slices (about 1/2 lb.)
   Canadian bacon
1 tablespoon chopped fresh
   thyme
1 tablespoon chopped fresh
   parsley
1/4 teaspoon salt
1/8 teaspoon pepper

1 tablespoon cornstarch
1/4 cup dry white wine

Place turkey breast skin-side down. Spread cut surfaces with mustard; top with Canadian bacon, thyme and parsley. Fold long sides of breast over stuffing so they overlap slightly. Skewer or tie to hold sides together. Sprinkle with salt and pepper. Place skin-side up on rack in slow-cooker. Cover and cook on LOW about 6 hours. Remove turkey and rack from pot; let juices remain. Keep covered and warm. Turn pot on HIGH. Dissolve cornstarch in wine. Stir into drippings in pot. Cover and cook on HIGH 20 to 30 minutes or until thickened, stirring occasionally. Remove skewer or tie from turkey. Slice turkey crosswise into 3/8- or 1/2-inch slices. Spoon wine sauce over slices. Makes 6 to 8 servings.

1 serving contains:

Cal	Prot	Carb	Fat	Chol	Sodium
241	43g	1g	6g	99mg	443mg

✤ *If fresh herbs are not available, substitute 1 teaspoon dried for each tablespoon fresh.*

Italian Roll-Ups

This will enhance your reputation as a hostess.

1/4 cup pine nuts, coarsely
  chopped
1 garlic clove, minced
2 tablespoons chopped fresh
  parsley
2 tablespoons chopped fresh
  basil
1 tablespoon olive
  or vegetable oil
1/4 teaspoon salt
1/8 teaspoon pepper
1-1/2 lbs. boneless round
  steak, about 1/2-inch thick
6 slices proscuitto, well
  trimmed
1 cup beef broth or bouillon
1 oz. dried porcini or shitake
  mushrooms
1/2 cup dry red wine

2 tablespoons cornstarch
1/4 cup cold water
Pine nuts

In small bowl, combine 1/4 cup chopped pine nuts, garlic, parsley, basil, oil, salt and pepper. Remove most of fat from steak. Cut into 6 pieces about 3" x 4". Pound to about 1/4-inch thickness or 4" x 6". Place a slice of proscuitto on each slice of pounded round steak. Spoon about 1 tablespoon herb mixture on each. Roll up like a jelly roll. Tie with string. Place on bottom of slow-cooker. Heat broth or bouillon to boiling. Pour over dried mushrooms. Add to cooker. Pour in wine. Cover; cook on LOW 6 to 7 hours. Remove meat; cover and keep warm. Turn pot on HIGH. Dissolve cornstarch in water. Stir into liquid in pot. Cover; cook on HIGH 15 to 20 minutes or until thickened. Spoon over roll-ups. Sprinkle with additional pine nuts. Makes 6 servings.

1 serving contains:

Cal	Prot	Carb	Fat	Chol	Sodium
326	36g	7g	15g	101mg	395mg

Sorrento Chicken

To make a very smooth sauce, process thickened broth in food processor just before spooning it over chicken.

1 tablespoon Dijon-style mustard

1/2 teaspoon chopped fresh tarragon

1 teaspoon minced fresh chives

1/4 teaspoon salt

1/8 teaspoon pepper

6 chicken breast halves, boned, skinned

1-1/2 oz. proscuitto, cut into 6 (1" x 9") strips

1 cup fresh pearl onions, peeled

1/2 cup dry white wine

1/2 cup chicken broth or bouillon

1 cup seasoned croutons

Combine mustard, tarragon, chives, salt and pepper. Spread on chicken breasts. Wrap strip of proscuitto around each. Place rack in bottom of slow-cooker. Top with wrapped chicken and onions. Combine wine and chicken broth or bouillon; pour over chicken. Cover and cook on LOW 5 to 6 hours or until chicken is tender. Remove chicken and rack; cover and keep warm. Turn pot on HIGH. Pulverize croutons in food processor until they look like brown sugar. Stir into broth mixture. Cover and cook on HIGH 15 to 20 minutes or until thickened. Spoon over cooked chicken breasts. Makes 6 servings.

1 serving contains:

Cal	Prot	Carb	Fat	Chol	Sodium
124	17g	5g	2g	41mg	315mg

❖ *This succulent dish reminds us of one we had in Sorrento, Italy.*

79

Mediterranean Ratatouille

Keep warm in a slow-cooker during a party. Let guests dip pita wedges into it. A versatile dish that can serve as a main dish, side dish or appetizer.

1 large eggplant, peeled, cubed

2 tomatoes, peeled, seeded, cubed

3 zucchini, cubed

1 small onion, chopped

1 yellow bell pepper, cubed

1/4 cup vegetable oil

1 garlic clove, crushed

1/4 cup chopped fresh cilantro leaves

2 tablespoons chopped fresh basil

1/2 teaspoon salt

1/4 teaspoon pepper

Pita bread, cut into wedges

Combine eggplant, tomatoes, zucchini, onion and bell pepper in slow-cooker. In small bowl, combine oil, garlic, cilantro, basil, salt and pepper. Add to vegetables in pot. Cover and cook on LOW 7 to 8 hours or until vegetables are tender. Use as a hearty vegetable dip or appetizer with pita bread. Makes 6 to 8 servings as a main dish; 20 to 25 as a dip.

1 serving contains:

Cal	Prot	Carb	Fat	Chol	Sodium
91	1g	7g	7g	0	140mg

Black Bean-Jalapeño Mousse

If your digestive system is jalapeño-friendly, use 2 jalapeño peppers. An excellent brunch dish that is tasty with grilled chicken and fresh fruit.

6 slices bacon, chopped

1 lb. dried black beans, rinsed

1 jalapeño pepper, seeded, chopped

1/2 teaspoon salt

1/4 teaspoon pepper

2 (10-1/2-oz.) cans beef broth

1 teaspoon instant beef bouillon

1 cup red wine vinegar

1 cup dry red wine

1 cup water

8 oz. smoked ham, diced

1 cup chopped fresh cilantro

1 large onion, chopped

2 envelopes unflavored gelatin

1/3 cup cold water

Goat Cheese Topping:

5 oz. goat cheese

1/4 cup dairy sour cream

1/3 cup nonfat milk

2 green onions, chopped

Stuffed green olives and fresh cilantro sprigs

Sauté bacon until crisp, drain; set aside. Spray 8-inch springform pan with no-stick cooking spray; set aside. Rinse beans; drain. Pour beans into slow-cooker. Top with jalapeño pepper, salt and pepper. In 3- or 4-quart saucepan, combine beef broth, bouillon, vinegar, wine, 1 cup water, ham, chopped cilantro, onion and bacon. Cover and cook on medium-high until mixture boils. Pour into slow-cooker; stir. Cover and cook on HIGH 6 hours or until beans are tender. When beans are tender, sprinkle gelatin over 1/3 cup water. When softened, stir into hot beans. Purée half of bean mixture at a time. Pour purée into springform pan; cover and refrigerate.

Goat Cheese Topping: Combine cheese, sour cream, milk and green onions; stir until well blended. Cover and refrigerate until serving time. To serve, remove side of springform pan; cut into wedges. Top with Cheese Topping; garnish with olives and cilantro, if desired. Makes 8 or 10 servings.

1 serving contains:

Cal	Prot	Carb	Fat	Chol	Sodium
272	21g	25g	9g	35mg	833mg

Persimmon Pudding

The bright orange, fig-shaped Hachiya persimmon should be very soft; the reddish-orange, tomato-shaped Fuyu can be slightly firm.

1-1/2 cups all-purpose flour
1 cup sugar
1 teaspoon baking powder
1 teaspoon baking soda
1 teaspoon cinnamon
1/4 teaspoon nutmeg
2 persimmons
1 tablespoon lemon juice
1/3 cup milk
1 egg
2 tablespoons honey
1/4 cup melted margarine or
  butter
1/2 cup chopped raisins
1/4 cup chopped pecans

Hot Citrus Sauce:
2 tablespoons cornstarch
1/2 cup sugar
1/2 cup water
1/2 cup orange juice
2 tablespoons margarine
1/4 teaspoon grated lemon
  peel
3 tablespoons lemon juice

Grease 6- or 8-cup heat-proof mold. In large bowl, combine flour, sugar, baking powder, soda, cinnamon and nutmeg; set aside. Cut persimmons in half; scoop out pulp. Purée lemon juice and pulp in blender or food processor fitted with metal blade. Add milk, egg, honey and margarine; process until well blended. Stir liquid into flour mixture. Add raisins and nuts. Spoon into mold; cover. Place on rack in slow-cooker. Pour in boiling water until it comes halfway up sides of mold. Cover and steam on HIGH 3 hours. Loosen sides by inserting a knife between pudding and sides of mold. Invert on a platter. Serve with Hot Citrus Sauce. Makes 6 to 8 servings.

Hot Citrus Sauce: In small saucepan, combine cornstarch and sugar. Add water and orange juice; stir until smooth. Stir over medium-low heat until thickened and translucent. Add margarine; stir until melted. Remove from heat. Stir in lemon peel and juice. Makes about 1-1/2 cups.

1 serving with sauce contains:

Cal	Prot	Carb	Fat	Chol	Sodium
414	5g	80g	10g	28mg	266

Holiday Cran-Apple Sauce

A very versatile dish! It's equally good as an accompaniment to poultry, dessert or breakfast fruit.

1 cup fresh cranberries
8 apples, peeled, cored, chopped
1/2 cup sugar
1 stick cinnamon, halved crosswise
6 whole cloves

Ground nutmeg

Combine cranberries, apples and sugar in slow-cooker. Place cinnamon and cloves in center of a 6-inch square of cheesecloth. Pull up around sides; tie to form pouch. Place in pot. Cover and cook on LOW 4 to 5 hours or until cranberries and apples are very soft. Remove spice bag. Purée hot fruit in blender or food processor fitted with metal blade. Sprinkle with nutmeg. Makes about 3-1/2 cups.

1 tablespoon contains:

Cal	Prot	Carb	Fat	Chol	Sodium
18	0	5g	0	0	0

Punch-of-Gold

The easiest punch you've ever made; keep it hot in the slow-cooker for guests to help themselves.

2 (12-oz.) cans apricot nectar
1 quart orange juice
1/4 cup orange liqueur
2 (12-oz.) cans mango nectar
3 pieces crystallized ginger, halved
2 cinnamon sticks

Fresh mint leaves

In slow-cooker, combine all ingredients except mint leaves. Cover; cook on LOW 4 or 5 hours. With slotted spoon, remove ginger and cinnamon sticks. Serve in punch cups or coffee mugs; garnish with mint leaves. Makes 15 to 18 servings.

1 serving contains:

Cal	Prot	Carb	Fat	Chol	Sodium
82	1g	18g	0	0	3mg

❖ *Keep slow-cooker on LOW to keep punch warm during the evening; this is ideal for buffet serving.*

Honey-Buttered Cranberry Cider

Try this bright, vibrantly flavored beverage. The slow-cooker keeps it hot until guests are ready for it.

1 (48-oz.) bottle cranberry juice cocktail

1 quart apple juice or cider

4 thin strips orange peel, about 2 inches long

1/3 cup margarine or butter

1/4 cup honey

1/2 teaspoon ground coriander

In slow-cooker, combine cranberry juice, apple juice or cider and orange peel. Cover and heat on LOW 5 to 7 hours. Just before serving, melt margarine or butter, honey and coriander in small saucepan or in microwave. Spoon slightly more than 1/2 tablespoon honey-margarine mixture in mug or heat-proof cup; add about 3/4 cup hot cranberry mixture. Serve immediately. Makes 12 to 15 servings.

1 serving contains:

Cal	Prot	Carb	Fat	Chol	Sodium
127	0	25g	3g	0	54mg

Fiesta Black-Bean Dip

Guests who enjoy more spicy foods will enjoy adding a bit of fresh or bottled salsa on each chip.

1 cup dried black beans, rinsed

1 quart water

1 onion, chopped

1 garlic clove, crushed

1/4 cup chopped fresh cilantro

1/4 teaspoon salt

1 fresh jalapeño pepper, seeded, chopped

1/4 lb. salt pork, coarsely chopped

2 or 3 oz. goat cheese, crumbled

Fresh cilantro leaves for garnish

Taco or tortilla chips

Salsa, optional

In slow-cooker, combine dried beans, water, onion, garlic, 1/4 cup chopped cilantro, salt, jalapeño pepper and salt pork. Cover and cook on LOW 9 to 10 hours or until beans are soft. Drain; discard water. In blender or food processor fitted with metal blade, process drained bean mixture until almost smooth. Spoon into serving bowl. Sprinkle cheese and fresh cilantro leaves over top. Dip chips into bean mixture. Top with salsa, if desired. Makes about 2-1/2 cups.

1 tablespoon contains:

Cal	Prot	Carb	Fat	Chol	Sodium
24	1g	2g	1g	2mg	55mg

Round-the-World Flavors

It's fun to borrow traditional flavors from other parts of the world. Good cooks in Europe have been "slow-cooking" for centuries. These early versions of slow-cookers were not electric, but heavy iron pots that simmered on the back of the stove or on the edge of a fireplace

Our round-the-world recipes are not designed to be authentic replicas of ethnic or regional dishes. Instead we used favorite flavor combinations that have been traditional for generations. Then we adapted them for use in slow-cooking.

Fr: France is famous for its fine food and unique flavor combinations. Savor the blend of spices in the classic Cassoulet, The Crockery Way. Sliced fresh mushrooms with a simple vinaigrette dressing makes an ideal salad. Crusty French bread complements the superb entrée.

MENU

*Cassoulet, The Crockery Way,
page 106
Fresh Mushroom Salad
French Bread
Apple Tart*

Slow-Cooker Tamale Pie

When serving, be sure to include part of cornmeal lining in addition to meat mixture in the center.

2 cups chicken broth
  or bouillon
1 cup yellow cornmeal
1 tablespoon chopped fresh
  cilantro
1/2 lb. pork sausage
1 lb. beef stew meat, cut into
  1/2-inch cubes
1 onion, chopped
1/2 cup finely chopped celery
1 mild green chile pepper,
  seeded, chopped
1/2 cup chopped sun-dried
  tomatoes
1 (8-oz.) can whole-kernel
  corn, drained
1 (2-1/2-oz.) can sliced ripe
  olives, drained
1/2 teaspoon salt
1/8 teaspoon pepper
Whole or halved pitted ripe
  olives, optional

Bring broth or bouillon to boil in medium saucepan. Stirring constantly, slowly add cornmeal. Simmer mixture 5 minutes, stirring occasionally. Stir in cilantro. Using a greased spatula, spread cornmeal mixture on bottom and about 2 inches up sides of slow-cooker. In large bowl, combine sausage, stew meat, onion, celery, chile pepper, sun-dried tomatoes, corn, sliced olives, salt and pepper. Carefully spoon into center of cornmeal-lined pot. Cover and cook on LOW 7 to 8 hours. Garnish with ripe olives, if desired. Makes 6 or 7 servings.

1 serving contains:

Cal	Prot	Carb	Fat	Chol	Sodium
372	24g	24g	20g	69mg	566mg

✤ *Do not remove cover during cooking because heat escapes quickly.*

Aegean Lamb and Eggplant on Fettuccine

Popular flavor combination of lamb and eggplant plus intriguing accents of sun-dried tomatoes and Feta cheese.

1 small eggplant, peeled, cut into 1-inch cubes

1 small onion, chopped

1/4 cup sun-dried tomatoes in oil, chopped

1/4 teaspoon dried red-pepper flakes

1 tablespoon balsamic vinegar

1/4 teaspoon salt

1 tablespoon chopped fresh basil

1 lb. lamb stew meat, cut into 2" x 1/2" strips

Cooked fettuccine

Feta cheese, crumbled

Fresh basil leaves

In slow-cooker, combine eggplant, onion, sun-dried tomatoes, red-pepper flakes, vinegar, salt, basil and lamb. Cover; cook on LOW 5 to 6 hours or until lamb is tender. Remove from cooker; spoon over cooked fettuccine. Top with crumbled feta cheese. Garnish with fresh basil leaves. Makes 4 to 5 servings.

1 serving contains:

Cal	Prot	Carb	Fat	Chol	Sodium
195	19g	4g	11g	61mg	156mg

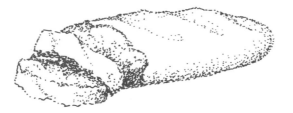

Taste-of-Thai Chicken Salad

Avoid the boning process by substituting 6 boneless chicken breast halves for the whole fryer.

1 (2-1/2- to 3-lbs.) chicken
1 cup chicken broth
1/2 teaspoon dry
   red-pepper flakes
1/2 teaspoon seasoned salt
1 tablespoon chopped fresh
   chives

1 cup snow peas
1 (8-oz.) can sliced water
   chestnuts, drained
1 red bell pepper, thinly sliced
1/4 cup vegetable oil
1 tablespoon sesame oil
1 tablespoon lime juice
2 tablespoons white wine
   vinegar
1 tablespoon soy sauce
2 teaspoons finely chopped
   fresh ginger root
Tabasco® sauce
1 garlic clove, crushed
1 orange, peeled, sliced
1/4 cup salted peanuts

Cut chicken in pieces; place in slow-cooker. In small bowl, combine broth, red-pepper flakes, seasoned salt and chives. Pour over chicken. Cover and cook on LOW 4 to 5 hours or until chicken is done. Cool; remove meat from bones. Cut meat into bite-size pieces. Discard bones; use broth for soup or stew. Blanch snow peas; cool. In large bowl, combine chicken, snow peas, water chestnuts and bell pepper. In small bowl, combine oils, lime juice, vinegar, soy sauce, ginger root, 3 or 4 dashes of Tabasco® and garlic. Add to chicken mixture; toss. Top with orange slices and sprinkle with chopped peanuts just before serving. Makes 5 or 6 servings.

1 serving contains:

Cal	Prot	Carb	Fat	Chol	Sodium
355	30g	12g	21g	79mg	446mg

✢ *Thai foods are often fragrant with spicy surprises and are always beautifully presented.*

Minestrone Napoli

A satisfying and delicious soup that is hearty enough to be used as a main dish.

3 large tomatoes, peeled, seeded, chopped

1 bunch green onions, chopped

2 medium carrots, peeled, chopped

1/4 cup chopped fresh parsley

1 garlic clove, crushed

2 tablespoons chopped fresh basil leaves

1 (15-oz.) can red kidney beans, drained

2 zucchini, sliced

2 cups shredded cabbage

1/2 teaspoon chopped fresh oregano

1/2 teaspoon salt

1/8 teaspoon pepper

5 cups beef broth or bouillon

1/4 cup dry red wine

2 cups cooked small elbow pasta

1/4 cup grated Parmesan cheese, optional

In slow-cooker, combine tomatoes, green onions, carrots, parsley, garlic, basil, kidney beans, zucchini, cabbage, oregano, salt, pepper, broth and wine. Cover and cook on LOW 8 to 9 hours. Stir in cooked pasta. Sprinkle with cheese, if desired. Makes 10 cups.

1 cup contains:

Cal	Prot	Carb	Fat	Chol	Sodium
113	6g	21g	1g	0	265mg

Greek Isles Pita Pockets

At your next party, keep the cooked shredded meat in your slow-cooker; guests will enjoy assembling everything.

1-1/2 lbs. lamb stew meat, cut into 1-inch cubes

3/4 lb. banana squash, peeled, cut into 1-inch cubes

1 medium red onion, diced

1/2 cup sliced celery

1/2 teaspoon salt

1 jalapeño pepper, seeded, minced

1 cube chicken bouillon, crushed or 1 teaspoon bouillon granules

1 garlic clove, crushed

1/8 teaspoon ground cumin

1/8 teaspoon ground coriander

8 to 10 pita bread rounds

8 to 10 lettuce leaves

1/4 cup (1 oz.) feta cheese, crumbled

1/4 cup plain yogurt

In slow-cooker, combine lamb, squash, onion, celery, salt, jalapeño pepper, bouillon, garlic, cumin and coriander. Cover and cook on LOW 8 to 9 hours or until meat is very tender. Strain mixture. Reserve about 1/4 cup broth; use remaining broth for soup or stew, if desired. Process drained cooked-meat mixture with reserved 1/4 cup broth in food processor until shredded. Cut about 1 inch off top of each pita round. Insert lettuce leaf into each. Spoon in meat mixture. Top with cheese and yogurt. Makes 8 to 10 servings.

1 serving contains:

Cal	Prot	Carb	Fat	Chol	Sodium
309	24g	38g	7g	54mg	654mg

✤ *Use caution when working with jalapeño or chile peppers; they can irritate your skin. Wear rubber gloves for protection if you have sensitive skin.*

Neopolitan Tostada

Halve each pita round horizontally to form 2 shell-like rounds; then toast just before serving.

3/4 lb. ground turkey
1 eggplant, cubed
1 cup fresh or canned salsa
1 (6-oz.) can tomato paste
1/4 cup chopped fresh parsley
1 tablespoon chili powder
1 teaspoon ground cumin
1 teaspoon dried oregano
1 (10-oz.) pkg. frozen corn, thawed

4 pita rounds, halved, toasted
1/2 cup plain lowfat yogurt
2 cups shredded lettuce
1/2 cup sliced ripe olives
1/2 cup shredded cheese, optional

Combine turkey, eggplant, salsa, tomato paste, parsley, chili powder, cumin, oregano and corn in slow-cooker. Cover and cook on LOW 5 to 6 hours. Stir with a fork to break up large chunks of turkey. Spoon about 3/4 cup cooked turkey mixture on each pita half. Top with yogurt, lettuce, olives and cheese, if desired. Makes 8 servings.

1 serving contains:

Cal	Prot	Carb	Fat	Chol	Sodium
256	16g	34g	8g	26mg	328mg

Old World Goulash

Flavors borrowed from our European heritage create this hearty dish.

**1-1/2 lbs. boneless beef chuck,
   cut into 1-inch cubes**

1 onion, sliced

2 teaspoons paprika

1/4 teaspoon salt

1/8 teaspoon pepper

1/2 cup beef broth or bouillon

**2 medium potatoes, peeled,
   shredded**

**1 (14-oz.) can sauerkraut,
   drained**

1 tablespoon brown sugar

1/4 teaspoon caraway seeds

**1/2 cup plain lowfat yogurt or
   dairy sour cream**

In slow-cooker, combine beef and onion. Sprinkle with paprika, salt and pepper. Pour broth or bouillon over all. Top with shredded potatoes, sauerkraut, brown sugar and caraway seeds. Cover and cook on LOW 8 to 9 hours. Turn off heat; stir in yogurt or sour cream. Makes 6 to 7 servings.

1 serving contains:

Cal	Prot	Carb	Fat	Chol	Sodium
265	25g	14g	12g	78mg	517

Provençale Smoked Sausage Ratatouille

This recipe is a cross between a stew and a soup; it contains our favorite flavors of southern France.

1 eggplant, peeled, cut into
   1/2-inch cubes

3 zucchini, cut into 1/2-inch
   slices

1 medium onion, sliced

2 medium tomatoes

1 large green bell pepper

1 large yellow bell pepper

1 jalapeño pepper

1 tablespoon chopped fresh
   basil

1/4 teaspoon salt

1 tablespoon minced parsley

1/2 lb. smoked link sausage,
   thinly sliced

2 cups chicken broth
   or bouillon

Combine eggplant, zucchini and onion in slow-cooker. With sharp knife, make an X in skin at smooth end of tomatoes. Drop in boiling water for about 15 seconds; pull off skin. Halve and remove tomato and bell pepper seeds. Cut tomatoes and bell peppers in 1/2-inch pieces; seed and finely chop jalapeño pepper. Add tomatoes, peppers, basil, salt, parsley, smoked sausage and broth or bouillon to slow-cooker. Stir; cover and cook on LOW 4 to 6 hours. Makes 7 to 8 servings.

1 serving contains:

Cal	Prot	Carb	Fat	Chol	Sodium
138	6g	8g	9g	20mg	357mg

Brazilian Feijoada

Not quite as elaborate as the traditional dish of Brazil but with similar flavors.

1 lb. dried black beans, rinsed
1 medium onion, chopped
1 garlic clove, crushed
2 tomatoes, peeled, seeded, chopped
1 tablespoon chopped jalapeño pepper
1 tablespoon chopped fresh parsley
1/4 lb. Canadian bacon in one piece
3 or 4 oz. beef jerky, cut each into 12ths
1 lb. smoked sausage links, cut each into 3rds
2 quarts water

2 oranges, peeled, thinly sliced
Cooked rice

In 5-quart slow-cooker, combine beans, onion, garlic, tomatoes, jalapeño pepper and parsley. Top with Canadian bacon, jerky and sausage. Pour water over all. Cover and cook on LOW 10 to 12 hours or until beans are tender. With slotted spoon, remove meat from slow-cooker. Scoop out about 3 cups beans with liquid. In blender or food processor fitted with metal blade, process these beans until almost smooth. Drain remaining beans; discard liquid. Combine puréed beans with drained beans. Spoon all beans on large platter. Slice Canadian bacon and sausage. Arrange jerky and sliced meat around side of platter. Serve with sliced oranges and cooked rice. Makes 10 to 12 servings.

1 serving contains:

Cal	Prot	Carb	Fat	Chol	Sodium
276	17g	23g	13g	39mg	518mg

New-Style Pozole

A delicious potpourri of flavors with overtones of the traditional recipe.

**1 lb. boneless pork shoulder,
  cubed**
1 lb. chicken thighs
2 slices bacon, chopped
1 small onion, chopped
1/2 teaspoon salt
**1 cup chicken broth
  or bouillon**
1 garlic clove, crushed
1 teaspoon chili powder
**2 (16-oz.) cans hominy,
  drained**
**1/4 teaspoon crushed dried
  red-pepper flakes**

Paprika

In slow-cooker, combine all ingredients except paprika. Cover and cook on LOW 6 to 7 hours or until meat is tender. With slotted spoon, remove chicken from pot; remove and discard bones. Cut chicken into slivers; return to pot. Refrigerate. When cold, skim and remove fat. Just before serving, heat in microwave or on stovetop. Sprinkle with paprika. Makes 8 to 10 servings.

1 serving contains:

Cal	Prot	Carb	Fat	Chol	Sodium
202	18g	12g	8g	58mg	207mg

✤ *In New Mexico, traditional pozole is served on Christmas Eve. Serve with crusty French bread or tortillas.*

Slow-Poke Jambalaya

Flavors that are typical of this classic Creole dish have plenty of time to mingle in the slow-cooker.

1 large red or green bell
    pepper, seeded, chopped
1 large onion, chopped
2 medium tomatoes, chopped
1 cup chopped celery
1 garlic clove, crushed
2 tablespoons minced fresh
    parsley
2 teaspoons chopped fresh
    thyme leaves
2 teaspoons chopped fresh
    oregano leaves
1/8 teaspoon cayenne
1/2 teaspoon salt
4 oz. smoked sausage,
    chopped
8 oz. chicken breast, skinned,
    boned, chopped
2 cups beef broth or bouillon

1/2 lb. cooked, shelled
    medium shrimp, halved
    lengthwise
1 cup cooked rice

In slow-cooker, combine all ingredients except shrimp and rice. Cover and cook on LOW 9 to 10 hours. Turn slow-cooker on HIGH; add cooked shrimp and cooked rice. Cover; cook on HIGH 20 to 30 minutes. Makes 7 to 8 servings.

1 serving contains:

Cal	Prot	Carb	Fat	Chol	Sodium
166	18g	9g	6g	90mg	369mg

Turkey Moussaka in Taco Shell

Make your own taco shells from corn tortillas or buy a package of ready-made ones; heat in microwave or oven.

3/4 lb. ground turkey
1 medium onion, chopped
4 mushrooms, sliced
1 garlic clove, crushed
1 (6-oz.) can tomato paste
1/2 cup dry white wine
1 tablespoon chopped parsley
1/2 teaspoon salt
1 teaspoon pickling spices
4 whole peppercorns

Yogurt Cream Sauce:
1 tablespoon margarine or
**   butter**
1 tablespoon all-purpose flour
1/8 teaspoon salt
1/3 cup milk
1 egg, beaten slightly
1/2 cup unflavored yogurt
1/16 teaspoon ground nutmeg

8 taco shells

In slow-cooker, combine turkey, onion, mushrooms, garlic, tomato paste, wine, parsley and salt. Tie pickling spices and peppercorns in cheesecloth bag or place them in a tea ball. Add to pot; cover and cook on LOW about 5 hours. Remove spice bag. Prepare Yogurt Cream Sauce. Spoon about 1/4 cup moussaka into each taco shell. Top with Yogurt Cream Sauce. Makes 8 tacos.

Yogurt Cream Sauce: In small saucepan or microwave, melt margarine or butter; stir in flour and salt. Gradually add milk. Cook and stir over low heat until thickened. Remove from heat. In small bowl, combine egg, yogurt and nutmeg. Stir into hot mixture in pan. Return to heat. Cook and stir over low heat 1 minute. Serve over moussaka.

1 taco contains:

Cal	Prot	Carb	Fat	Chol	Sodium
199	12g	17g	9g	50mg	310mg

Coq Au Vin

Slow-cooker version of classic French dish of chicken with wine.

1 (2-1/2- to 3-lb.) chicken,
   cut up
2 slices bacon, cooked,
   drained, chopped
4 shallots, peeled, sliced
1 garlic clove, crushed
1 tablespoon chopped fresh
   parsley
1 bay leaf
1/2 teaspoon chopped fresh
   thyme
1/4 teaspoon salt
1/8 teaspoon pepper
15 small white boiling onions
10 mushrooms, halved
1/2 cup dry red wine
1/2 cup chicken broth or
   bouillon
1 plum tomato, peeled,
   seeded, finely chopped

2 tablespoons cornstarch
2 tablespoons cold water

Place chicken in slow-cooker. Add cooked bacon, shallots, garlic, parsley, bay leaf, thyme, salt, pepper, onions, mushrooms, wine, broth or bouillon and tomato. Cover and cook on LOW 8 to 9 hours. Remove chicken and vegetables with slotted spoon. Discard bay leaf. Turn pot on HIGH. Dissolve cornstarch in water; stir into juices in pot. Cover; cook on HIGH 20 to 30 minutes, stirring occasionally. Pour over chicken mixture. Makes about 5 servings.

1 serving contains:

Cal	Prot	Carb	Fat	Chol	Sodium
367	47g	10g	13g	136mg	321mg

✤ *A welcome dish for any time of the year.*

Tortilla Stack

Thanks to convenience foods, this dish is easily put together and delicious tasting.

1-1/2 lbs. lean ground beef
8 corn tortillas, each cut into
**   6 wedges**
1 can Cheddar cheese soup,
**   undiluted**
1 pkg. taco seasoning mix
**   (dry)**
3 medium tomatoes, chopped

1/4 cup dairy sour cream
2 cups shredded lettuce
1/4 cup chopped green onion
1 red bell pepper, chopped
1 avocado, peeled, chopped

Crumble one-fourth of ground beef into bottom of slow-cooker. Top with one-fourth of tortilla wedges. In small bowl, combine soup and taco mix. Spread one-fourth of soup mixture over tortillas in pot. Sprinkle with one-fourth of tomatoes. Repeat layering until all ingredients are in pot. Cover and cook on LOW 4 to 5 hours.

Spoon onto individual plates. Top each serving with sour cream, and shredded lettuce, green onions, bell pepper and avocado. Makes 6 or 7 servings.

1 serving contains:

Cal	Prot	Carb	Fat	Chol	Sodium
372	21g	25g	23g	67mg	387mg

Moroccan Hens

For a more authentic North African menu, substitute couscous for rice.

**2 Cornish hens, thawed,
   halved**
1 garlic clove, crushed
1 tablespoon honey
1/4 teaspoon ground turmeric
1 teaspoon grated onion
1/2 teaspoon ground allspice
1/4 teaspoon salt
1/16 teaspoon cayenne
**1 large tomato, peeled,
   seeded, chopped**

Cooked rice
**1 tablespoon toasted sesame
   seeds**

Rinse hens; pat dry. In small bowl, combine garlic, honey, turmeric, onion, allspice, salt and cayenne. Brush on chicken; cover and refrigerate at least 4 hours. Place in slow-cooker with juice from marinade; sprinkle tomatoes over top. Cover; cook on LOW 5-1/2 to 6 hours. Arrange on serving plate over cooked rice. Sprinkle with toasted sesame seeds. Makes 4 servings.

1 serving contains:

Cal	Prot	Carb	Fat	Chol	Sodium
240	32g	7g	9g	94mg	217mg

Alsatian-Style Choucroute

Slow-cooker version of the meal-in-a-dish that's a tradition in the Alsace area of France.

27 to 30 oz. refrigerated
  or canned sauerkraut
1 medium cooking apple,
  peeled, seeded, chopped
1 medium onion, chopped
1 carrot, shredded
8 juniper berries
1 bay leaf
1 tablespoon chopped fresh
  parsley
3 pork chops, boned, halved
6 slices (about 1/2 lb.)
  Canadian bacon
1/2 lb. smoked sausage,
  cut into 6 or 8 pieces
1/4 lb. hot Italian sausage,
  sliced
1/2 cup dry white wine
1 cup chicken broth
  or bouillon

Cooked new potatoes

Drain sauerkraut in colander or strainer. Rinse; drain again. In slow-cooker, arrange alternate layers of drained sauerkraut, apple, onion and carrot. Tie juniper berries, bay leaf and parsley in cheese-cloth; add to pot. Top with pork chops, Canadian bacon, smoked sausage and Italian sausage. Pour wine and chicken broth or bouillon over ingredients in pot. Cover and cook on LOW 6 to 8 hours. Remove and discard spice bag. With slotted spoon, place sauerkraut and vegetables in center of large platter. Arrange meats over and around vegetables. Serve with cooked new potatoes. Makes 6 to 8 servings.

1 serving contains:

Cal	Prot	Carb	Fat	Chol	Sodium
277	19g	9g	17g	63mg	1320mg

Italian-Style Bean Soup

You may be surprised if the mushrooms turn dark, but you'll like the flavor.

**1 cup small dried white beans,
   rinsed**
**6 cups chicken broth
   or bouillon**
1 onion, chopped
1/2 cup chopped fennel
**1 teaspoon chopped fresh
   thyme**
1 bay leaf
**6 mushrooms, coarsely
   chopped**
1/4 teaspoon pepper
**2 oz. (about 1/3 cup)
   prosciutto, chopped**

1/4 cup dry white wine
Fennel leaves

In slow-cooker, combine beans, broth or bouillon, onion, chopped fennel, thyme, bay leaf, mushrooms, pepper and prosciutto. Cover and cook on LOW 7 to 8 hours or until beans are tender. Remove and discard bay leaf. Stir in wine. Garnish each serving with a sprig of fennel. Makes 6 or 7 servings.

1 serving contains:

Cal	Prot	Carb	Fat	Chol	Sodium
132	11g	16g	2g	5mg	117mg

Cassoulet, The Crockery Way

Mild Italian sausage can be substituted if you prefer a less spicy dish.

1 lb. dried great Northern
    beans, rinsed
1 large onion, chopped
1/4 teaspoon pepper
1 garlic clove, crushed
1 tablespoon chopped fresh
    parsley
2 whole cloves
1 bay leaf
1 sprig fresh thyme
1/4 lb. salt pork, diced
1 lb. boneless lamb, cut into
    1-inch cubes
1/2 lb. hot Italian sausage,
    crumbled
2 medium tomatoes, peeled,
    seeded, chopped
3 cups beef broth or bouillon
1 cup dry red wine

In slow-cooker, combine beans, onion, pepper, garlic and parsley. Wrap cloves, bay leaf and thyme in cheesecloth or metal tea container. Add to pot. Add salt pork, lamb, sausage and tomatoes. Pour beef broth or bouillon and wine over all. Cover; cook on LOW 9 to 10 hours. Remove and discard spice bag. Makes 6 to 7 servings.

1 serving contains:

Cal	Prot	Carb	Fat	Chol	Sodium
483	39g	31g	20g	92mg	473mg

✤ *Several villages in Southwest France insist they originated Cassoulet (ka su lay). Despite the controversy we all enjoy this hearty dish.*

Slow-Cooker & Other Appliances

Your slow-cooker doesn't replace other appliances; it teams up with them to produce a wide variety of dishes. The microwave is handy for making sauces to go over dishes made in the slow-cooker. It can be used to reheat cooked meat and/or vegetables that you take out of the slow-cooker while you're thickening a sauce. Also the oven or toaster oven is handy for toasting nuts, pita rounds and sesame seeds.

Pasta and rice can simmer in a conventional pan on the stovetop before they're drained and added to other ingredients in the slow-cooker near the end of cooking.

Broil your favorite fish and transform it into a great dish by topping it with our Southwestern Sauce. Make the sauce ahead and quickly reheat in your microwave. Subtly flavored spaghetti squash and a crisp green salad complete your meal. Serve scrumptious Piña Colada Bread Pudding either warm or cold.

MENU

Broiled Fish
Southwestern Sauce, page 111
Spaghetti Squash
Green Salad
Blue Corn Muffins
Piña Colada Bread Pudding,
page 41

Turkey Lasagne

A classic favorite with turkey replacing traditional ground beef.

3/4 lb. ground turkey
1 small onion, chopped
1/2 cup chopped green
   or red bell pepper
1 garlic clove, crushed
2 (8-oz.) cans tomato sauce
1 (14-1/2-oz.) can ready-cut
   peeled tomatoes
1 teaspoon chicken bouillon
   granules or 1 bouillon cube
1 teaspoon chopped fresh
   oregano leaves
1/4 teaspoon salt
1/8 teaspoon pepper

1/2 lb. lasagne noodles
8 oz. ricotta cheese
8 oz. mozzarella cheese, sliced

In slow-cooker, combine turkey, onion, bell pepper, garlic, tomato sauce, tomatoes, bouillon, oregano, salt and pepper. Cover and cook on LOW 7 to 8 hours. Cook lasagne noodles according to package directions; drain. Preheat oven to 350F (175C). In 13" x 9" baking dish, arrange alternate layers of cooked lasagne noodles, hot turkey-tomato mixture, ricotta cheese and mozzarella cheese. Bake in preheated oven 30 minutes or until bubbly around edges. Makes 6 to 8 servings.

1 serving contains:

Cal	Prot	Carb	Fat	Chol	Sodium
324	24g	30g	13g	49mg	830mg

Tropic Treasure Baby Back Ribs

A happy blend of traditional American seasonings with flavors of the tropics.

1 tablespoon grated fresh
   ginger root
1 garlic clove, crushed
2 tablespoons honey
1/2 teaspoon ground
   coriander
1/2 teaspoon ground turmeric
1/4 cup soy sauce
2 tablespoons white wine
   vinegar
1/4 cup ketchup
1/4 teaspoon salt
4 or 5 drops Tabasco® sauce
1 teaspoon instant chicken
   bouillon or 1 chicken
   bouillon cube, crumbled
4 to 5 lbs. baby back pork
   ribs, cut into 2- or 3-rib
   pieces

2 teaspoons sesame seeds

In small bowl, combine ginger root, garlic, honey, coriander, turmeric, soy sauce, vinegar, ketchup, salt, Tabasco® and bouillon. Brush both sides of ribs with sauce. Place in slow-cooker. Pour remaining sauce over all. Cover and cook on LOW 6 to 7 hours or until tender. With fork or slotted spoon, lift ribs from slow-cooker. Place single layer of drained ribs in shallow baking pan; brush with drippings in pot. Sprinkle with sesame seeds. Broil in oven until sesame seeds begin to brown. Makes 6 to 8 servings.

1 serving contains:

Cal	Prot	Carb	Fat	Chol	Sodium
375	26g	8g	26g	103mg	891mg

Southwestern Sauce

Use a 1-quart Crock-Ette® for this recipe or double the recipe and make it in a 3-1/2- or 4-quart pot. You can keep sauce in refrigerator for a week, then reheat it at serving time.

4 medium tomatoes, peeled, seeded, chopped

3 medium tomatillos, husked, chopped

1 tablespoon vegetable oil

1 tablespoon minced green onions

1 jalapeño pepper, seeded, chopped

1 garlic clove, crushed

1 tablespoon red wine vinegar

1 tablespoon chopped fresh cilantro

1/4 teaspoon salt

Broiled fish or chicken
Fresh cilantro leaves

In 1-quart slow-cooker, combine tomatoes, tomatillos, oil, onions, jalapeño pepper, garlic, vinegar, 1 tablespoon cilantro and salt. Cover and cook on LOW 3-1/2 to 4 hours. Spoon over broiled fish or chicken. Garnish with cilantro leaves. Makes about 2-3/4 cups sauce.

1 tablespoon contains:

Cal	Prot	Carb	Fat	Chol	Sodium
7	0	1g	0	0	17mg

❖ *You'll find many uses for this sauce: topping broiled fish or poultry, adding zest to beans, roast beef or lamb sandwiches.*

111

Stuffed Onions, Southeast-Asia Style

Use the scooped-out pieces of onion to season other vegetable or meat dishes.

5 medium onions, peeled
1/2 lb. ground turkey
1/2 cup soft breadcrumbs
1 egg, beaten slightly
1 garlic clove, crushed
1 tablespoon soy sauce
1 tablespoon hoisin sauce
1/4 teaspoon ground ginger

Plum Glaze:
1/2 cup plum jelly
1 tablespoon white wine
    vinegar
1 tablespoon ketchup
1 teaspoon Dijon-style
    mustard
Toasted sesame seeds

With sharp knife, cut about 1/2-inch slice across top of each onion. Carefully cut out centers, leaving about 1/2-inch sides and bottom. In medium bowl, combine turkey, breadcrumbs, egg, garlic, soy sauce, hoisin sauce and ginger. Spoon about 1/4 cup stuffing into each onion shell. Place rack in slow-cooker, add 1/2 cup water. Arrange filled onions on rack. If all onions do not fit on bottom of cooker, place 3 on bottom; lightly cover with heavy-duty foil. Arrange remaining onions on top. Cover and cook on LOW 7 to 8 hours or until onions are tender. Spoon Plum Glaze over onions. Makes 5 servings.

Plum Glaze: At serving time, combine jelly, vinegar, ketchup and mustard. Stir over low heat or in microwave until dissolved. Spoon over cooked onions. Sprinkle with sesame seeds.

1 serving contains:

Cal	Prot	Carb	Fat	Chol	Sodium
219	12g	29g	7g	69mg	380mg

Refried Beans (Frijoles)

Guaranteed to be a hit as accompaniment to enchiladas, tacos or other Mexican dishes.

1 lb. dried pinto beans, rinsed
1/4 teaspoon dried
   red-pepper flakes
1 garlic clove
1/4 lb. salt pork, cubed
6 cups water
1/2 teaspoon salt, optional

1 tablespoon vegetable oil

Shredded Cheddar cheese,
   optional

In slow-cooker, combine dried beans, red-pepper flakes, garlic, salt pork and water. Cover and cook on LOW 10 to 11 hours. Add salt, if desired. Partially mash beans with potato masher or in food processor. Serve now or refrigerate. Just before serving, heat oil in large skillet. Add beans; heat and stir until fairly dry. Top with cheese or serve plain. Makes 7-1/2 cups.

1 cup contains:

Cal	Prot	Carb	Fat	Chol	Sodium
226	12g	31g	6g	6mg	123mg

Stuffed Acorn Squash

Use "hot" or "regular" sausage, depending on your tolerance for spicy foods.

2 acorn squash, halved, seeded
1 tablespoon vegetable oil
1/2 lb. bulk sausage
1 egg, beaten slightly
3 slices raisin bread, toasted,
  coarsely crumbled
1/4 teaspoon ground nutmeg
1/2 teaspoon Dijon-style
  mustard
1 orange, peeled, cut into 4
  crosswise slices

Orange-Nutmeg Sauce:
1 tablespoon cornstarch
1 cup orange juice
1 tablespoon honey
1 teaspoon lemon juice
Ground nutmeg

Brush cut edges and inside squash with oil. In small bowl, combine sausage, egg, toasted bread, nutmeg and mustard. Spoon into squash halves. Place cut-side up on rack in slow-cooker. Top each with slice of orange. Cover pot, cook on LOW 5 to 6 hours or until squash is tender. Spoon Orange-Nutmeg Sauce over all. Makes 4 servings.

Orange Nutmeg-Sauce: In small saucepan or microwave dish, dissolve cornstarch in orange juice. Cook over moderate heat or in microwave until thickened. Stir in honey and lemon juice. Spoon over cooked squash. Sprinkle with nutmeg.

1 serving contains:

Cal	Prot	Carb	Fat	Chol	Sodium
529	13g	60g	29g	92mg	481mg

Curried Carrot Bisque

Mouth-watering flavors plus an appetizing golden color guarantee a hit.

8 medium carrots, peeled, chopped
1 onion, chopped
1 cooking apple, peeled, chopped
1 teaspoon curry powder
1 garlic clove, crushed
1/4 teaspoon ground coriander
1/8 teaspoon allspice
1/4 teaspoon salt
3 cups chicken broth or bouillon

1 cup milk or light cream
Chopped fresh cilantro leaves

In slow-cooker, combine carrots, onion, apple, curry powder, garlic, coriander, allspice, salt and broth or bouillon. Cover and cook on LOW 9 to 10 hours or until carrots are very tender. Purée, half at a time, in blender or food processor fitted with metal blade. Gradually stir in milk or cream. Reheat in microwave or in saucepan on stove. Sprinkle cilantro on top. Makes about 6 cups.

1 cup contains:

Cal	Prot	Carb	Fat	Chol	Sodium
98	5g	16g	2g	4mg	143mg

✤ *Although there is a herb that's called* curry plant, *the curry powder we're familiar with is a blend of many spices. Turmeric supplies the deep-golden color.*

Turkey Trot Stew

Baked Cheddar Topping is delicious on Barbecued Beans 'n Beef, page 141 or Beef 'n Turkey Sausage Chili, page 29.

1 lb. dried black-eye peas,
   rinsed
2 cups chicken broth
   or bouillon
4 cups water
1 teaspoon ground coriander
1/2 teaspoon ground cumin
1 teaspoon ground cardamom
1 onion, chopped
1/8 teaspoon dried
   red-pepper flakes, crushed
1/2 teaspoon salt
2 (about 1-1/2-lbs.) turkey
   thighs, skinned

Baked Cheddar Topping:
1-1/2 cups boiling water
1/4 teaspoon salt
2/3 cup yellow cornmeal
1 egg, beaten slightly
4 tablespoons dairy sour
   cream
3/4 cup shredded Cheddar
   cheese

In slow-cooker, combine dried peas, broth or bouillon and water. Stir in coriander, cumin, cardamom, onion, red-pepper flakes and salt. Place thighs on top of dried peas and seasonings. Cover and cook on LOW 9 to 10 hours or until peas are tender. Remove thighs; cut meat into small chunks or shreds. Discard bones. Place meat and stew in casserole. Prepare Baked Cheddar Topping.

Baked Cheddar Topping: In medium saucepan, combine water and salt; gradually stir in cornmeal. Cook, stirring constantly, about 5 minutes or until thick. Remove from heat. Preheat oven to 375F (190C). Mix egg, sour cream and cheese. Gradually stir in cooked cornmeal. Drop in 9 mounds on top of cooked mixture in casserole. Bake 25 to 35 minutes or until topping begins to brown. Makes 8 to 9 servings.

1 serving contains:

Cal	Prot	Carb	Fat	Chol	Sodium
296	24g	30g	9g	69mg	280mg

Vegetable Smoothie

Use your slow-cooker to prepare this dish the day before you're entertaining; then heat it in the oven just before serving.

5 medium potatoes, peeled, quartered

1 medium celery root, peeled, cubed

1 medium leek, trimmed, cut into 1/2-inch crosswise slices

1/2 teaspoon salt

1/8 teaspoon pepper

1/4 teaspoon seasoned salt

4 cups water

1/2 cup milk or half and half

1 egg, slightly beaten

1 tablespoon minced parsley

1/4 cup melted margarine or butter

In slow-cooker, combine potatoes, celery root, leek, salt, pepper, seasoned salt and water. Cover and cook on LOW 6 to 7 hours or until tender. Drain; mash with electric mixer or food processor fitted with metal blade. Add milk or half and half, egg, parsley and 3 tablespoons melted margarine or butter. Spoon into 1-1/2-quart baking dish. Drizzle top with remaining tablespoon of melted margarine or butter. Bake in preheated 350F (175C) oven 25 to 30 minutes or until slightly browned on top. Makes 6 servings.

1 serving contains:

Cal	Prot	Carb	Fat	Chol	Sodium
197	5g	30g	7g	37mg	456mg

Almond Ginger Apples

The meringue topping makes an interesting presentation but may be omitted, if desired.

6 large apples
1/4 cup almond paste
2 tablespoons powdered sugar
1 tablespoon minced crystallized ginger
1/4 teaspoon grated lemon peel
1/4 cup chopped toasted almonds

1 egg white
1/8 teaspoon lemon juice
1 tablespoon granulated sugar
2 tablespoons slivered almonds

With vegetable peeler, remove apple cores. In small bowl, combine almond paste, powdered sugar, ginger, lemon peel and chopped almonds. Spoon into center of each apple. Place in slow-cooker. If all apples do not fit on bottom of cooker, place 3 on bottom; lightly cover with heavy-duty foil. Arrange remaining apples on top of foil. Cover and cook on LOW 4 to 5 hours or until apples are done.

Just before serving, in small mixing bowl, beat egg white and lemon juice until foamy. Gradually beat in granulated sugar until peaks are stiff but not dry. Swirl on top of cooked apples. Place apples in broiler pan; sprinkle with slivered almonds. Broil until brown on top. Serve immediately. Spoon juice from slow-cooker over top, if desired. Makes 6 servings.

1 serving contains:

Cal	Prot	Carb	Fat	Chol	Sodium
182	3g	30g	7g	0	11mg

Cook Today—Serve Tomorrow

There are times when foods take all day or night to cook. As a result, it is important to consider when to start the cooking process so you don't have to get out of bed in the middle of the night to turn the pot off.

The foods in this chapter are cooked, then chilled before serving. That's good reason to let them cook one day, then refrigerate overnight for serving the next day. These cold soups and main-dish salads are welcome additions to summertime menus.

This homey menu combines our favorite Barbecued Beef Sandwiches and Traditional Baked Beans and promises you a carefree weekend. Prepare Barbecued Beef the day before; reheat in your microwave. Start your beans the night before and let them cook while you sleep. Cap the meal with fresh corn and rhubarb pie, which remind us of summer's bounty.

MENU

Barbecued Beef Sandwiches,
page 124
French Rolls
Corn on the Cob
Traditional Baked Beans, page 61
Rhubarb Pie

Cold Green Vichyssoise

Plan ahead for adequate time to refrigerate this dish several hours or overnight.

5 medium potatoes, peeled, cut into 8ths

2 leeks, washed, sliced crosswise

1/4 cup fresh basil leaves

1 (10-oz.) pkg. frozen chopped spinach, thawed, drained

1/4 cup watercress leaves

3 cups chicken broth or bouillon

1/2 teaspoon seasoned salt

2 cups milk

1/2 teaspoon salt

1/8 teaspoon pepper

1 cup light cream
Fresh basil springs for garnish

In slow-cooker, combine potatoes, leeks, basil, spinach, watercress, broth or bouillon, seasoned salt, milk, salt and pepper. Cover and cook on LOW 6 to 7 hours or until vegetables are very tender. Purée in blender or food processor fitted with metal blade. Add light cream; refrigerate until cold. Ladle into individual bowls. Garnish with basil sprigs. Makes 8 servings.

1 serving contains:

Cal	Prot	Carb	Fat	Chol	Sodium
206	8g	28g	8g	26mg	283mg

❖ *Spinach and watercress supply both color and flavor.*

Cup-of-Gold Refresher

Cook this soup the night before, refrigerate it during the day, then serve it cold for dinner.

**3 apples, peeled, cored,
   chopped**
6 carrots, peeled, chopped
1 small onion, chopped
**1 tablespoon margarine or
   butter**
2 teaspoons curry powder
1/8 teaspoon ground allspice
1/4 teaspoon salt
1/8 teaspoon pepper
**3 cups chicken broth
   or bouillon**

1/2 cup dairy sour cream
**2 tablespoons toasted slivered
   almonds**

In slow-cooker, combine apples, carrots, onions, margarine or butter, curry powder, allspice, salt, pepper and broth or bouillon. Cover and cook on LOW 9 to 10 hours or until vegetables are very soft. Purée, half at a time, in blender or food processor fitted with metal blade. Refrigerate at least 3 hours or until chilled. Stir in sour cream. Sprinkle with toasted almonds. Makes about 6 cups.

1 cup contains:

Cal	Prot	Carb	Fat	Chol	Sodium
161	5g	20g	8g	9mg	148mg

❖ *Smooth, cool and flavorful describes this wonderful, warm-weather dish.*

Cold Summer Squash Soup

A refreshing cold soup to make when summer squash is at the peak of garden-fresh flavor.

**3 medium crookneck squash,
  sliced**
3 medium zucchini, sliced
**2 tablespoons sliced green
  onions**
1 garlic clove, crushed
1/2 teaspoon salt
1/8 teaspoon pepper
**3 cups chicken broth
  or bouillon**

**1/4 cup loosely packed
  watercress leaves**
**1/2 cup plain lowfat yogurt,
  stirred**
1/4 teaspoon dried dill weed

Watercress sprigs for garnish

In slow-cooker, combine crookneck squash, zucchini, green onions, garlic, salt, pepper and broth or bouillon. Cover and cook on LOW 7 to 8 hours or until squash is very tender. In blender or food processor fitted with metal blade, purée hot vegetable mixture with watercress, yogurt and dill until smooth. Chill several hours or overnight. Serve in individual bowls; garnish with watercress sprigs. Makes 6 servings.

1 serving contains:

Cal	Prot	Carb	Fat	Chol	Sodium
50	4g	6g	1g	2mg	194mg

Barbecued Beef Sandwiches

The meat may be cooked a day ahead and refrigerated overnight. Skim solidified fat from top of sauce and meat. Reheat beef, shred and spoon on rolls.

2-1/2 to 3 lbs. lean boneless chuck roast

3/4 cup tomato ketchup

1 tablespoon Dijon-style mustard

2 tablespoons brown sugar

1 garlic clove, crushed

1 tablespoon Worcestershire sauce

2 tablespoons red wine vinegar

1/4 teaspoon liquid smoke flavoring

1/4 teaspoon salt

1/8 teaspoon pepper

10 to 12 French rolls or sandwich buns

Place beef in slow-cooker. Combine remaining ingredients, except rolls. Pour over meat. Cover and cook on LOW 8 to 9 hours. Refrigerate or prepare sandwiches now. Shred beef by pulling it apart with 2 forks; add 1 cup sauce. Reheat mixture in microwave or on stovetop. Spoon on warm, open-face rolls or buns. Top with additional warm sauce, if desired. Makes 10 to 12 servings.

1 serving contains:

Cal	Prot	Carb	Fat	Chol	Sodium
420	29g	42g	14g	75mg	711mg

Smoked Turkey and Bean Salad

Add a crunchy French roll and a glass of iced tea for a successful summer luncheon.

1 cup dried pinto beans, rinsed

1 cup dried garbanzo beans, rinsed

1/4 lb. smoked turkey, diced

4 cups water

2 tablespoons chopped fresh parsley

1 garlic clove, crushed

1 cup cooked green beans, drained

1/2 cup olive oil

1/4 cup white wine vinegar

1 tablespoon Dijon-style mustard

2 teaspoons honey

2 tablespoons chopped fresh chives

1/2 teaspoon dried dill weed

1/4 teaspoon salt

1/8 teaspoon pepper

1 small cucumber, peeled, diced

1/4 cup loosely packed watercress leaves

Lettuce

Chopped pimiento

In slow-cooker, combine dried beans, turkey, water, parsley and garlic. Cover; cook on LOW 10 to 11 hours or until beans are tender but firm.

Drain and discard liquid; cool drained bean mixture. Add green beans. In medium bowl, combine oil, vinegar, mustard, honey, chives, dill, salt and pepper. Pour over bean mixture; chill. Stir in cucumber and watercress. Serve in lettuce-lined bowl. Sprinkle with chopped pimiento. Makes 6 or 7 servings.

1 serving contains:

Cal	Prot	Carb	Fat	Chol	Sodium
319	12g	30g	18g	7mg	277mg

Antipasto Bean Salad

Serve with sliced salami and mortadella plus a loaf of Italian bread.

1 lb. dried pink beans, rinsed
6 cups chicken broth
  or bouillon
1 garlic clove, crushed
1/4 cup chopped celery leaves

1/2 cup olive oil
1/4 cup vegetable oil
1/3 cup white wine vinegar
1/4 cup loosely packed
  chopped basil
4 anchovy filets, chopped
1 red onion, thinly sliced
2 medium tomatoes, chopped
1/4 cup sliced ripe olives
1/2 teaspoon salt
1/8 teaspoon pepper

Lettuce leaves
1/4 cup (1 oz.) Gorgonzola
  cheese, crumbled

The day before serving, combine dried beans, broth or bouillon, garlic and celery leaves in slow-cooker. Cover and cook on LOW 9 to 10 hours or until beans are tender. Drain; refrigerate beans several hours or overnight. Discard liquid. In large bowl, toss chilled beans with oils, vinegar, basil, anchovies, onions, tomatoes, olives, salt and pepper. Spoon into lettuce-lined bowls or plates. Sprinkle with Gorgonzola cheese. Makes 7 to 8 servings.

1 serving contains:

Cal	Prot	Carb	Fat	Chol	Sodium
398	15g	33g	24g	6mg	311mg

Pinto Pepper Salad

This colorful salad never fails to win admiration.

1 lb. dried pinto beans, rinsed
6 cups water

1 yellow or green bell pepper,
seeded, chopped
1 fresh mild green chile
or jalapeño pepper, seeded,
finely chopped
1 small red onion, diced
2 cups cherry tomatoes,
halved
1 cup thinly sliced fennel
2 cups bottled Italian salad
dressing

Lettuce
Hard-cooked eggs

In slow-cooker, combine dried beans and water. Cover and cook on LOW 9 to 10 hours or until beans are done. Remove beans with slotted spoon; discard liquid and refrigerate beans until chilled. In large bowl, combine drained beans, bell pepper, chile or jalapeño pepper, onion, tomatoes and fennel. Add salad dressing; toss. Serve on lettuce. Garnish with wedges of hard-cooked eggs. Makes 7 or 8 servings.

1 serving contains:

Cal	Prot	Carb	Fat	Chol	Sodium
449	10g	39g	36g	0	482mg

Black Bean Vinaigrette

When buying ham hocks, try to find meaty ones with a minimum of fat.

1 lb. dried black beans, rinsed
7 cups water
2 ham hocks or 1 cup
   chopped ham
1 garlic clove, crushed
2 fresh jalapeño peppers,
   seeded, chopped

3/4 cup olive or vegetable oil
1/3 cup red wine vinegar
1/2 cup chopped red or
   yellow bell pepper
2 tablespoons chopped fresh
   parsley
1/4 cup chopped green onion
1/2 teaspoon salt
2 tablespoons capers

Lettuce leaves
2 hard-cooked eggs, chopped

The day before serving, combine dried beans, water, ham, garlic and jalapeño peppers in slow-cooker. Cover and cook on LOW 8 to 9 hours or until beans are tender. Cool to room temperature or refrigerate overnight. Drain thoroughly; discard liquid. If using ham hocks, chop lean meat; discard bones, skin and fat. In small bowl, combine oil, vinegar, bell pepper, parsley, green onion, salt and capers. Pour over beans; toss. Spoon into lettuce-lined bowl. Sprinkle eggs on top. Makes 6 to 8 servings.

1 serving contains:

Cal	Prot	Carb	Fat	Chol	Sodium
397	16g	29g	25g	64mg	435mg

✤ *Black beans, also called* turtle beans, *have been a staple in Mexico and countries to the south.*

Zippy Vegetable Dip

If you're short of time, substitute packaged tortilla chips for pita or tortillas.

2 medium eggplants, peeled,
 cubed
1/4 cup sun-dried tomatoes
 in oil, drained, chopped
1 garlic clove, crushed
1 onion, chopped
1 tablespoon chopped fresh
 Italian parsley
1/2 teaspoon chopped fresh
 thyme
1 tablespoon vegetable oil
1/2 teaspoon salt
1/4 teaspoon pepper
1/4 teaspoon crushed, dried
 red-pepper flakes

1/2 cup plain yogurt
2 teaspoons toasted sesame
 seeds
1/4 cup sliced ripe olives
Wedges of toasted pita rounds
 or corn tortillas

In slow-cooker, combine eggplants, tomatoes, garlic, onions, parsley, thyme, oil, salt, pepper and red-pepper flakes. Cover and cook on LOW 6 or 7 hours or until vegetables are soft. With slotted spoon, scoop eggplant mixture into blender or food processor fitted with metal blade. Process until smooth. Stir in yogurt. Spoon into shallow bowl; sprinkle with sesame seeds. Garnish with olives. Scoop on wedges of toasted pita bread or tortillas. Makes 3-1/4 cups dip.

1 tablespoon contains:

Cal	Prot	Carb	Fat	Chol	Sodium
14	0	2g	1g	0	28mg

Farmer's Pride Relish

If fresh corn is not available, use 2/3 cup frozen kernels and enjoy this old-time relish any time of the year.

2 ears corn
1 large green or red bell
  pepper, seeded, coarsely
  chopped
1 onion, chopped
2 cups thinly sliced cabbage
1/2 teaspoon dried
  red-pepper flakes
2/3 cup white wine vinegar
1/3 cup sugar
1/2 teaspoon curry powder
1/2 teaspoon ground
  coriander
1/4 teaspoon ground turmeric
1 teaspoon dry mustard
1/2 teaspoon salt

Cut corn off cob. Combine in slow-cooker with bell pepper, onion, cabbage, red-pepper flakes, vinegar, sugar, curry powder, coriander, turmeric, dry mustard and salt. Cover; cook on LOW 6 to 7 hours. Cool and serve as an accompaniment to chicken or pork. Makes about 3-1/2 cups.

1 tablespoon contains:

Cal	Prot	Carb	Fat	Chol	Sodium
9	0	2g	0	0	20mg

Winter Chutney

An unusual accompaniment to roast duck, chicken or pork.

3 pears, peeled, seeded, cut into chunks
1 cup dried   fruit bits
2 tablespoons sliced green onion
2 tablespoons lemon juice
1 cup sugar
1 teaspoon grated lemon peel
1/4 teaspoon crushed dried red-pepper flakes
1-1/2 teaspoon slivered crystallized ginger

Combine in slow-cooker pears, dried fruit, green onions, lemon juice, sugar, lemon peel, red-pepper flakes and ginger. Cover and cook on LOW 3 to 4 hours. Cool. Makes about 3 cups chutney.

1 tablespoon contains:

Cal	Prot	Carb	Fat	Chol	Sodium
28	0	7g	0	0	1mg

❖ *Chutney is a relish that orginated in East India. It usually combines sweet and sour ingredients. Both fruits and vegetables are teamed with herbs, spices and other seasonings.*

Quick and Easy

Are you so busy getting the family off to school and work that there's practically no time left to make any dinner preparation before you leave for work? Then this section of the book is designed for you. There's a minimum of time-consuming pre-preparation to worry you.

Thanks to a variety of convenience foods, much of the tedious work is done for you. A package of pork chops or chicken pieces turns into a culinary marvel with very little time and effort on your part.

These recipes take the normal amount of cooking time in a slow-cooker, but the preparation time is shorter than usual.

How many times have you wished for a tasty, yet quick and easy meal? The answer is orange-flavored Sunshine Drumsticks or you may choose Shortcut Spareribs. Quickly cook frozen mixed vegetables and toss a salad while muffins heat. Top the meal off with chocolate cake.

MENU

Sunshine Drumsticks, page 139
Tossed Green Salad
Mixed Vegetables
Whole-wheat Muffins
Chocolate Cake

Shortcut Spareribs

For a more crispy texture, place single layer of cooked and drained ribs in shallow baking pan; broil in oven until brown on edges.

3 to 4 lbs. pork spareribs
1 cup bottled barbecue sauce
1 (1/2-oz.) pkg. dry green onion dip mix

Cut spareribs into individual ribs; place in slow-cooker. Combine barbecue sauce and green onion dip mix. Spoon over ribs. Cover and cook on LOW 6 to 7 hours or until ribs are tender. With fork or slotted spoon, lift ribs to platter. Makes 4 to 6 servings.

1 serving contains:

Cal	Prot	Carb	Fat	Chol	Sodium
494	34g	7g	36g	137mg	953mg

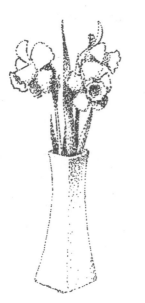

Crockery Cooker Fajitas

If you prefer poultry, substitute 1 to 1-1/2 lbs. chicken or turkey, skinned and boned for the beef.

1 to 1-1/2 lbs. boneless beef round steak, cut in strips

1 red bell pepper, cut in strips

1 large onion, cut into thin wedges

1 (1-oz.) pkg. dry fajita mix

1/4 cup water

6 or 7 (7- or 8-inch) flour tortillas

2 small tomatoes, chopped

1 avocado, peeled, thinly sliced

1/2 cup dairy sour cream

In slow-cooker, combine beef, bell pepper, onion, fajita mix and water. Cover and cook on LOW 5 to 6 hours or until meat is tender. Warm tortillas in microwave or conventional oven. With slotted spoon, lift meat mixture out of pot. Place about 3/4 cup mixture along center of each tortilla. Top with chopped tomato, avocado and sour cream. Fold both sides over filling. Makes 6 or 7 servings.

1 serving contains:

Cal	Prot	Carb	Fat	Chol	Sodium
292	19g	22g	15g	54mg	155mg

✤ *Don't expect these fajitas to be "sizzling" and crunchy brown like those in many restaurants, but they are tender and tasty.*

Easy Sweet-Sour Pork Chops

For a change of pace, substitute chicken breasts for this quick-to-fix pork dish.

1 (16-oz.) bag frozen
   Oriental-style vegetables,
   partially thawed
6 (about 2-1/4 lbs.) pork chops
1 (2-oz.) pkg. sweet-sour sauce
   blend mix
1/2 cup water

1 cup Chinese pea pods

Place partially thawed vegetables in slow-cooker. Arrange pork chops on top. Combine sauce mix and water. Pour sauce over chops and vegetables in slow-cooker. Cover and cook on LOW 7 to 8 hours. Turn on HIGH; add pea pods. Cover and cook on HIGH about 5 minutes. Makes 6 servings.

1 serving contains:

Cal	Prot	Carb	Fat	Chol	Sodium
205	21g	12g	8g	58mg	69mg

Potato Leek Chicken Thighs

Leek soup mix creates a sauce that emphasizes the basic flavor created by the sliced fresh leek.

5 medium potatoes, peeled, sliced

1 medium leek, washed, thinly sliced

10 to 12 chicken thighs

1 (1.8-oz.) pkg. leek soup mix

1 cup cold water

Combine potatoes and leek. Place on bottom of slow-cooker. Arrange chicken over potatoes. In small bowl, combine leek soup mix and water. Whisk until well mixed. Pour over chicken. Cover; cook on LOW 5 to 6 hours or until chicken is tender. Makes 5 to 6 servings.

1 serving contains:

Cal	Prot	Carb	Fat	Chol	Sodium
442	34g	30g	20g	116mg	874mg

❖ *Serve with sliced tomatoes and hot biscuits.*

Sunshine Drumsticks

For a stronger citrus flavor, add 1 (8 oz.) can drained mandarin oranges to cooked sauce.

12 chicken drumsticks, skinned

1 (6-oz. or 12-oz.) can frozen orange juice concentrate, thawed, not reconstituted

2 to 3 tablespoons honey

2 tablespoons quick-cooking tapioca

1 fresh mild green chile or jalapeño pepper, seeded, thinly sliced

1/4 teaspoon salt

1 teaspoon dried onion flakes

Place chicken in slow-cooker. In small bowl, combine orange juice concentrate, honey, tapioca, chile or jalapeño pepper, salt and onions. Pour over chicken. Cover and cook on LOW about 5 hours or until tender. Spoon sauce over chicken. Makes 12 drumsticks.

1 drumstick contains:

Cal	Prot	Carb	Fat	Chol	Sodium
152	15g	12g	6g	48mg	92mg

✚ *Adjust the flavorings to your personal taste. Use the higher range of orange juice, honey and jalapeño for extra orange flavor, spice or sweetness.*

Honey-Mustard Barbecued Short Ribs

Start with bottled barbecue sauce or your favorite sauce recipe, then add a few additional flavors to perk up short ribs.

3 to 3-1/2 lbs. beef short ribs
1 tablespoon Dijon-style mustard
1 garlic clove, crushed
2 tablespoons honey
1/2 teaspoon salt
1/8 teaspoon pepper
1 cup bottled hickory smoke barbecue sauce

2 tablespoons cornstarch
2 tablespoons cold water

Cooked noodles

Place short ribs in slow-cooker. In medium bowl, combine mustard, garlic, honey, salt, pepper and barbecue sauce. Pour over ribs. Cover and cook on LOW 6 to 7 hours or until tender. Refrigerate several hours or overnight. Skim any solidified fat from top. Remove ribs; heat in microwave or conventional oven. Dissolve cornstarch in cold water. Add to sauce from ribs. Cook and stir in microwave or on stovetop until hot and slightly thickened. Pour hot sauce over warm ribs. Serve on cooked noodles. Makes 6 to 8 servings.

1 serving contains:

Cal	Prot	Carb	Fat	Chol	Sodium
349	35g	9g	18g	102mg	507mg

Barbecued Beans 'n Beef

So easy to put together with canned beans and bottled barbecue sauce.

1-1/2 lbs. round steak or beef stew meat, cut into 1/2-inch cubes

1 onion, chopped

1/2 cup finely chopped celery

1 yellow or green bell pepper, seeded, chopped

2 (15-oz.) cans pinto beans, drained

1/4 teaspoon salt

1 cup bottled hickory smoke barbecue sauce

1 cup (4 oz.) grated Cheddar cheese, optional

In slow-cooker, combine all ingredients except cheese. Cover; cook on LOW 7 to 8 hours or until meat is tender. Top with grated cheese, if desired. Makes 6 to 8 servings.

1 serving contains:

Cal	Prot	Carb	Fat	Chol	Sodium
314	30g	32g	8g	61mg	363mg

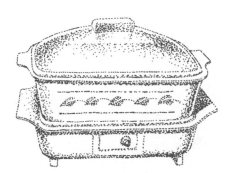

Picante Tomato Pizazz

*Use mild or hot picante sauce depending on your tolerance for hot,
spicy foods.*

1 (8-oz.) jar picante sauce
**1/4 cup loosely packed
  cilantro leaves**
2 quarts tomato juice
2 cups beef broth or bouillon

In blender or food processor fitted with metal blade, combine picante sauce and cilantro. Process until smooth. Pour into slow-cooker with tomato juice and broth or bouillon. Cover; cook on LOW 4 to 5 hours. Stir well; serve in mugs or coffee cups. Makes 9 or 10 servings.

1 serving contains:

Cal	Prot	Carb	Fat	Chol	Sodium
46	2g	9g	1g	0	728mg

✤ *A warm spicy drink, ideal for
  warming you on those cold days.*

"No Chopping" Vegetable Soup

For variety and convenience, use thin strips of pork or beef that many supermarkets sell for stir-frying.

2 cups beef broth or bouillon

1 (14-oz.) can stewed tomatoes

1 (16-oz.) can kidney beans, drained

1 (10-oz.) pkg. frozen mixed vegetables

1 (10-oz.) pkg. frozen baby onions

1 lb. fresh boneless turkey strips

1 teaspoon chili powder

1/2 teaspoon salt

1/8 teaspoon pepper

1 cup crushed tortilla chips

In slow-cooker, combine all ingredients except tortilla chips. Cover; cook on LOW 8 or 9 hours or until vegetables are done. Serve in individual bowls; sprinkle with tortilla chips. Makes 7 to 8 servings.

1 serving contains:

Cal	Prot	Carb	Fat	Chol	Sodium
217	23g	22g	4g	39mg	497mg

Hot Baja Coffee

You can be assured that this specially flavored coffee stays hot in your slow-cooker.

8 cups hot water
3 tablespoons instant coffee granules
1/2 cup coffee liqueur
1/4 cup Crème de Cacao liqueur

3/4 cup whipped cream
2 tablespoons grated semi-sweet chocolate

In slow-cooker, combine hot water, coffee granules and liqueurs. Cover and heat on LOW 2 to 4 hours. Ladle into mugs or heat-proof glasses. Top with whipped cream and grated chocolate. Makes 10 to 12 servings.

1 serving contains:

Cal	Prot	Carb	Fat	Chol	Sodium
98	0	9g	3g	10mg	10mg

❖ *This delightful drink is good enough to be called* dessert.

Double-Corn Dumplings

A topping added to cooked food in a slow-cooker; then cooked covered on HIGH in the slow-cooker.

3/4 cup all-purpose flour
1/4 cup yellow cornmeal
2 teaspoons baking powder
1/8 teaspoon salt
1/2 cup fresh corn kernels
1/2 cup milk
2 tablespoons vegetable oil

In medium bowl, combine flour, cornmeal, baking powder and salt. Stir in corn, milk and oil. Spoon on cooked hot stew or chili in slow-cooker. Cover and cook on HIGH 30 to 35 minutes.

1 serving contains:

Cal	Prot	Carb	Fat	Chol	Sodium
85	2g	12g	3g	1mg	100mg

Index